MAIN COURSES

by
Jean Paré

Dedication

The star attraction - main course.

Cover Photo

MAIN COURSES

Fourteenth Printing March 1997

ISBN 0-9693322-1-1

Published and Distributed by
Company's Coming Publishing Limited
Box 8037, Station "F"
Edmonton, Alberta, Canada
T6H 4N9

**Published Simultaneously in
Canada and the United States of America**

Printed In Canada

Company's Coming Cookbooks
by Jean Paré

table of Contents

the Jean Paré story

Jean Paré grew up understanding that the combination of family, friends and home cooking is the essence of a good life. From her mother she learned to appreciate good cooking, while her father praised even her earliest attempts. When she left home she took with her many acquired family recipes, her love of cooking and her intriguing desire to read recipe books like novels!

In 1963, when her four children had all reached school age, Jean volunteered to cater to the 50th anniversary of the Vermilion School of Agriculture, now Lakeland College. Working out of her home, Jean prepared a dinner for over 1000 people which launched a flourishing catering operation that continued for over eighteen years. During that time she was provided with countless opportunities to test new ideas with immediate feedback—resulting in empty plates and contented customers! Whether preparing cocktail sandwiches for a house party or serving a hot meal for 1500 people, Jean Paré earned a reputation for good food, courteous service and reasonable prices.

"Why don't you write a cookbook?" Time and again, as requests for her recipes mounted, Jean was asked that question. Jean's response was to team up with her son, Grant Lovig, in the fall of 1980 to form Company's Coming Publishing Limited. April 14, 1981, marked the debut of "150 DELICIOUS SQUARES", the first Company's Coming cookbook in what soon would become Canada's most popular cookbook series. By 1995, sales had surpassed ten million cookbooks.

Jean Paré's operation has grown from the early days of working out of a spare bedroom in her home to operating a large and fully equipped test kitchen in Vermilion, Alberta, near the home she and her husband Larry built. Full-time staff has grown steadily to include marketing personnel located in major cities across Canada plus selected U.S. markets. Home Office is located in Edmonton, Alberta where distribution, accounting and administration functions are headquartered in the company's own 20,000 square foot facility. Growth continues with the recent addition of the Recipe Factory, a 2700 square foot test kitchen and photography studio located in Edmonton.

Company's Coming cookbooks are now distributed throughout Canada and the United States plus numerous overseas markets, all under the guidance of Jean's daughter, Gail Lovig. The series is published in English and French, plus a Spanish language edition is available in Mexico. Soon the familiar and trusted Company's Coming style of recipes will be available in a variety of formats in addition to the bestselling soft cover series.

Jean Paré's approach to cooking has always called for quick and easy recipes using everyday ingredients. She continues to gain new supporters by adhering to what she calls "the golden rule of cooking": never share a recipe you wouldn't use yourself. It's an approach that works—*ten million times over!*

Foreword

The main course you choose for a meal is given the starring role while the other dishes form the supporting cast. Your concern is to ensure that your production is a success.

Meat or poultry may be roasted covered or uncovered, as you prefer. Tender cuts lend themselves to roasting without a cover, especially if cooking rare to medium. Leaving the lid off encourages browning. Less tender cuts generally require covering to stay moist during the longer cooking period. The lid may be removed for browning up to a half hour before removing from the oven.

A meat thermometer takes the guess work out of cooking times. Be sure that it is in the center of the meat, not touching a bone. A thin roast cooks faster than a chunky roast of the same weight while tender well-aged meat cooks faster than meat not aged as long. Roasts continue to cook (for about 15 minutes) when removed from the oven. While the roast stands, use a wire whisk to make lump-free gravy.

Skin may be removed from chicken or turkey pieces before cooking or may be left on as desired. A few recipes specifically call for it to be removed. Turkey and chicken are interchangeable, although pieces would need to be the same size so as to cook the same length of time.

If you catch your own fish, you will be hard pressed to find a more economical main course. Fish cooks very quickly as it is not dense and has very little connective tissue. Fish and seafood lose their translucent color and most turn milky-white when cooked. Fish fillets of one type can be interchanged for another. Fresh fish may be used instead of canned or frozen if you are fortunate enough to have access to it.

For recipes requiring wine or sherry, alcohol-free versions may be used to give an authentic flavor.

Condiments are often served with the main course. Horseradish, mustard sauce and mustard are good with beef; applesauce with pork, goose and duck; cranberry sauce with chicken, turkey and other poultry. Pineapple and varieties of mustard are equally delicious served with ham. Lemon or lime wedges and tartar sauce are excellent with fish. Use condiments sparingly so as not to mask the delicious flavor of the main course.

So do you have any ideas about wat to serve for dinner tonight? Read on, and set the stage for MAIN COURSES!

Jean Paré

SEAFOOD CRÊPES

Shrimp and scallops combine to make this luncheon favorite topped with a delicious crab sauce.

Butter or margarine	¼ cup	60 mL
Finely chopped onion	¼ cup	60 mL
Sliced mushrooms	½ cup	125 mL
All-purpose flour	¼ cup	60 mL
Salt	½ tsp.	2 mL
Pepper	⅛ tsp.	0.5 mL
Chicken bouillon powder	½ tsp.	2 mL
Milk	1½ cups	350 mL
Canned broken shrimp, drained	4 oz.	113 g
Scallops, cooked and cut up	¼ lb.	113 g
Crêpes, see page 15	12	12

CRAB SAUCE

Butter or margarine	2 tbsp.	30 mL
All-purpose flour	2 tbsp.	30 mL
Salt	½ tsp.	2 mL
Milk	1 cup	225 mL
Crabmeat, drained, cartilage removed	4¾ oz.	135 g

Grated medium Cheddar
  cheese, for garnish

Melt butter in large saucepan. Add onion and mushrooms. Sauté until soft.

Mix in flour, salt, pepper and bouillon powder. Stir in milk until it boils and thickens. Remove from heat.

Add shrimp and scallops. Stir. Divide mixture among crêpes spooning lengthwise near center. Roll. Place seam side down in baking dish large enough to hold in single layer.

Crab Sauce: Melt butter in saucepan. Mix in flour and salt. Stir in milk until it boils and thickens.

Add crab. Stir and heat through. Add more milk if too thick. Spoon over crêpes.

Sprinkle with cheese. Cover. Bake in 350°F (180°C) oven for about 15 to 20 minutes until hot. Serves 6 people, 2 crêpes each.

Pictured on page 125.

SEAFOOD WELLINGTON

A delicious way to serve salmon enclosed in puff pastry. To give a shiny finish to pastry, brush with beaten egg before baking.

Butter or margarine	½ cup	125 mL
Finely chopped onion	½ cup	125 mL
Chopped fresh mushrooms	1 cup	250 mL
All-purpose flour	½ cup	125 mL
Parsley flakes	¾ tsp.	4 mL
Salt	½ tsp.	2 mL
Pepper	⅛ tsp.	0.5 mL
Milk	1¼ cups	300 mL
Salmon fillets (red is best)	1½ lbs.	675 g
Boiling salted water, to cover		
Frozen puff pastry, thawed	1 lb.	454 g

Melt butter in frying pan. Add onion and mushrooms. Sauté until soft.

Mix in flour, parsley, salt and pepper. Stir in milk until it boils and thickens. It will be very thick. Cool.

Poach salmon in salted water until it flakes. Remove from water. Cool. Divide into 4 servings.

Roll out pastry. Divide into 4 pieces. Spoon ⅛ sauce on pastry, lay salmon over, spoon ⅛ sauce on salmon. Bring up pastry. Fold over. Seal. Place seam side down on baking pan. Repeat. Cut 2 vents in top of each. Use scrap pieces of pastry to make fish cut-outs to place on top. Bake in 400°F (200°C) oven until browned, about 20 to 25 minutes. Serve with a dollop of Cucumber Sauce (page 40). Serves 4.

SARDINES CRISP

Almost as easy as eating from the can.

Sardines, drained	3½ oz.	100 g
Fine dry bread crumbs	2 tbsp.	30 mL
Margarine (butter browns too fast)	2 - 4 tbsp.	30 - 60 mL

Dip sardines into bread crumbs. Brown in margarine in frying pan. Serves 1 or 2.

FRUIT AND SEAFOOD KABOBS

Excellent for a main course or side dish. Most attractive and colorful.

Fresh medium size shrimp	18	18
Fresh medium size scallops	18	18
Boiling salted water, to cover		
Dried pitted prunes, stewed	12	12
Dried pitted apricots, stewed	12	12
Maraschino cherries	12	12
Butter or margarine, melted (butter is best)	¼ cup	60 mL

Cook shrimp and scallops separately in salted water. Simmer about 5 minutes. Shrimp will turn pink and scallops will turn milky white.

Prunes and apricots should be cooked according to package directions but not so they fall apart. Drain cherries well.

Arrange on 6 skewers. Lay skewers on baking sheet with sides. Chill until needed. Brush with melted butter and heat in 425°F (220°C) oven for about 5 to 10 minutes until piping hot. Serves 6.

Pictured on page 107.

BAKED STUFFED SALMON

Impressive! A great way to serve a whole fish.

Butter or margarine	¼ cup	60 mL
Grated carrot	1 cup	250 mL
Chopped onion	½ cup	125 mL
Chopped fresh mushrooms (optional)	½ cup	125 mL
Parsley flakes	1 tsp.	5 mL
Salt	½ tsp.	2 mL
Pepper	⅛ tsp.	0.5 mL
Dry bread crumbs	1½ cups	375 mL
Poultry seasoning	½ tsp.	2 mL
Water, as needed		
Whole salmon, head and tail removed	4½ lbs.	2 kg

(continued on next page)

Melt butter in frying pan. Add next 6 ingredients. Sauté until onion is soft and clear.

Put bread crumbs and poultry seasoning into bowl. Mix. Add onion-carrot mixture. Stir together.

Add water to moisten.

Grease large piece of foil. Lay salmon on top. Stuff cavity. Measure thickest part, then fold foil over to seal. Place on baking sheet. Bake in 450°F (230°C) oven allowing 10 minutes per 1 inch (2.5 cm) of thickness, measured at thickest part. Fish should flake easily when fork tested. Transfer to platter. Peel off top skin. Serve with Lemon Sauce (page 42) or Tartar Sauce (page 41). Serves 8 to 10.

DECORATED SALMON: To decorate and serve cold, omit stuffing. Put 2 celery ribs coarsely cut, 2 medium carrots cut in fingers and 1 small onion sliced into cavity and bake as above. Discard celery and carrots before decorating. Very thin lemon slices make a good covering. Mayonnaise can be piped to decorate, using a sliced olive for an eye.

CURRIED COD

Curry and tomatoes spice this up. No fat added.

Frozen cod fillets (or other fish), thawed	1 lb.	454 g
Canned tomatoes	1 cup	250 mL
Chopped onion	½ cup	125 mL
Chopped celery	¼ cup	60 mL
Parsley flakes	1 tsp.	5 mL
Curry powder	1 tsp.	5 mL
Garlic powder	⅛ tsp.	0.5 mL
Granulated sugar	1 tsp.	5 mL
Salt	¼ tsp.	1 mL

Lay fillets in single layer in greased saucepan.

Mix remaining ingredients together. Bring to a boil over medium heat. Simmer until onion is cooked. Pour over fish. Bake uncovered in 350°F (180°C) oven approximately 20 minutes or until fish flakes easily when fork tested. Serves 2 to 3.

FISH PIE

Not all cream pies are desserts!

Milk	2 cups	500 mL
Fish fillets (sole or other)	2 lbs.	1 kg
Butter or margarine	3 tbsp.	50 mL
All-purpose flour	3 tbsp.	50 mL
Salt	1 tsp.	5 mL
Pepper	1/4 tsp.	1 mL
Worcestershire sauce	1/2 tsp.	2 mL
Reserved milk	1 1/2 cups	375 mL
Cooked pie shell, 10 inch (23 cm)	1	1
Paprika, sprinkle		

Heat milk in saucepan. Add fish. Poach (simmer slowly) until barely cooked, until it flakes easily when fork tested, about 5 minutes. With slotted spoon lift out fish. Place on rack. Reserve milk.

Melt butter in another saucepan. Mix in flour, salt, pepper and Worcestershire sauce. Add reserved milk, stirring until it boils and thickens.

Put fish into pie shell. Pour cream sauce over top. Sprinkle with paprika. Bake uncovered in 350°F (180°C) oven for 5 to 10 minutes until browned. Cut into 6 wedges.

BROWN FISH

A very different way to serve fish which you will enjoy especially if you catch your own.

Fish steaks or fillets	4	4
Mayonnaise	3/4 cup	175 mL
Sour cream	1/4 cup	60 mL
Envelope dry onion soup	1	1
Oregano	1/2 tsp.	2 mL
Basil	1/2 tsp.	2 mL

Lay out fish in foil lined pan.

Mix remaining ingredients together. Spread over top of fish. Bake uncovered in 450°F (230°C) oven for about 15 minutes. Serves 4.

Fun to experiment. Try your own catch or any favorite fish.

Biscuit mix	2 cups	500 mL
Milk	½ cup	125 mL
Tomato sauce	7½ oz.	213 g
Oregano	¼ tsp.	1 mL
Basil	¼ tsp.	1 mL
Parsley flakes	½ tsp.	2 mL
Onion powder	¼ tsp.	1 mL
Seasoned salt	1 tsp.	5 mL
Shredded mozzarella cheese	2 cups	500 mL
Cooked fish fillets, broken up	½ lb.	225 g
Chopped green onion	¼ cup	60 mL
Sliced fresh mushrooms	5 - 8	5 - 8
Finely chopped green peppers	⅓ cup	75 mL
Grated Parmesan cheese	¼ cup	60 mL
Grated medium Cheddar cheese	1 cup	250 mL

Mix biscuit mix with milk to form soft ball. Pat into greased 12 inch (30 cm) pizza pan. Bake in 375°F (190°C) oven for 15 minutes to partially cook. Cool to handle.

In small bowl combine next 6 ingredients. Smooth over crust.

Layer remaining ingredients in order given. Add more Cheddar cheese if desired. Return to oven for 15 minutes or until very hot and cheese is melted. To bake in a large quiche dish, press dough up the side of dish. After baking for 5 minutes remove from oven and press dough into shape flattening bottom and sides. Continue baking for another 10 minutes. Cuts into 6 or 8 wedges.

Note: To make a more substantial main course, add 1 lb. (454 g) cooked fish.

Pictured on page 71.

Paré Pointer

All baby zombies love stuffed animals, especially their deady bear.

FISH FILLETS WITH SHRIMP

An extra special treat. Looks nice and tastes fantastic.

Frozen fish fillets, thawed	1 lb.	454 g
SHRIMP SAUCE		
Butter or margarine	3 tbsp.	50 mL
All-purpose flour	3 tbsp.	50 mL
Salt	1/2 tsp.	2 mL
Pepper	1/8 tsp.	0.5 mL
Milk	1 cup	250 mL
Mayonnaise	1/4 cup	60 mL
Small or broken shrimp, drained	4 oz.	113 g
Paprika, sprinkle		

Arrange fish in single layer in greased baking dish.

Shrimp Sauce: Melt butter in saucepan over medium heat. Mix in flour, salt and pepper. Stir in milk and mayonnaise until it boils and thickens. Gently stir in shrimp. Pour over fish.

Sprinkle with paprika. Bake uncovered in 325°F (160°C) oven until fish flakes easily when fork tested, about 15 minutes. Serves 4.

TUNA RING

Keep these ingredients on the shelf for a simple and tasty dish.

Eggs	3	3
Tuna, drained and flaked	2 x 7 oz.	2 x 198 mL
Dry bread crumbs	1 1/2 cups	375 mL
Finely minced onion	1/4 cup	60 mL
Milk	1/2 cup	125 mL
Lemon juice	1 tbsp.	15 mL
Salt	1 tsp.	5 mL
Pepper	1/4 tsp.	1 mL

Beat eggs with fork in bowl. Add remaining ingredients. Mix together. Pack into greased 4 cup (1 L) ring mold. Bake uncovered in 350°F (180°C) oven for about 30 to 40 minutes. Ring will test done if you insert a knife and it comes out clean. Serve with Blue Cheese Sauce (page 41). Serves 5 to 6.

Pictured on page 89.

Once the crêpes are made the rest is quick to prepare.

Condensed cream of mushroom soup	10 oz.	284 mL
Condensed cream of chicken soup	10 oz.	284 mL
Crabmeat	1 lb.	500 g
Crêpes, see below	12	12
Paprika, sprinkle (optional)		

Stir both soups together in bowl. Add crabmeat. Mix together.

Using about ⅔ of mixture, divide among crêpes. Roll. Place seam side down in pan large enough to hold in single layer. Spoon remaining sauce over top. Sprinkle with paprika. Bake uncovered in 325°F (160°C) oven for 25 to 30 minutes until hot. Serves 6.

Pictured on page 125.

CRÊPES

Eggs	2	2
Milk	1¼ cups	300 mL
All-purpose flour	1 cup	250 mL
Cooking oil	2 tbsp.	30 mL
Salt	½ tsp.	2 mL

In small mixing bowl beat all ingredients together until batter is smooth. Let stand for 1 hour. Lightly grease 7 inch (18 cm) crêpe or frying pan. Heat over quite high heat. Put 2 to 3 tbsp. (30 to 45 mL) batter into pan swirling and tipping pan to spread. If batter is too thick add a bit more milk. When browned, turn to brown other side. If crêpes are made by dipping crêpe pan into batter only 1 side is browned. Makes about 18.

Paré Pointer

If a jeweller married a person who ran a laundry would you have a ring around the collar?

SHRIMP NEWBURG

Make ahead and store in refrigerator or freezer. Serve with garlic or cheese toast and a green salad or serve over rice.

Butter or margarine	¼ cup	60 mL
Chopped onion	1 cup	250 mL
Sliced mushrooms	1 cup	250 mL
All-purpose flour	¼ cup	60 mL
Salt	½ tsp.	2 mL
Milk	1½ cups	375 mL
Tomato sauce	3 tbsp.	50 mL
Lemon juice	1 tsp.	5 mL
Cooked shrimp	1 lb.	500 g
Sour cream	½ cup	125 mL
Sherry (or alcohol-free sherry)	2 tbsp.	30 mL

Melt butter in frying pan. Add onion and mushrooms. Sauté until onion is soft and clear.

Mix in flour and salt. Add milk, tomato sauce and lemon juice. Heat and stir until it boils and thickens.

Add shrimp, sour cream and sherry. Turn into 2 quart (2 L) casserole. Bake uncovered in 350°F (180°C) oven for about 30 minutes until bubbling hot. Serves 4.

1. Steak Diane page 59
2. Lobster Tails page 24

CRAB CAKES

These delicate tender cakes are a delight to eat.

Crabmeat	1 lb.	500 g
Egg	1	1
Dry onion flakes, crushed	1 tbsp.	15 mL
Salt	½ tsp.	2 mL
Pepper	¼ tsp.	1 mL
Cracker crumbs	½ cup	125 mL
Mayonnaise	2 tbsp.	30 mL
Worcestershire sauce	½ tsp.	2 mL

Cracker crumbs, for coating

Mix first 8 ingredients together. Shape into patties.

Coat with remaining cracker crumbs. Cook in well greased frying pan browning both sides. Serve with lemon wedges. Makes 10 patties. Serves 5.

STUFFED FILLETS IN FOIL

No clean-up with this one. Stuffing goes well and is very tasty.

Dry bread crumbs	1 cup	250 mL
Onion flakes	1 tbsp.	15 mL
Parsley flakes	1 tsp.	5 mL
Poultry seasoning	¼ tsp.	1 mL
Salt	¼ tsp.	1 mL
Pepper, light sprinkle		
Water	3 tbsp.	50 mL
Butter or margarine, melted	3 tbsp.	50 mL
Fish fillets (sole, cod, perch or other)	1 lb.	454 g

Mix first 8 ingredients together to make stuffing.

Lay out first ½ fillets on foil. Cover with stuffing. Lay second ½ fillets over top. Fold foil up to seal. Place carefully on baking sheet. Bake in 375°F (190°C) oven for about 25 minutes. Serves 3.

Variation: Cut a partially frozen block of fish into 2 layers. Put stuffing between layers. Seal and bake about 30 minutes. Serves 3.

SALMON ROLLS

Try this for a different approach to good eating. A scrumptious mixture in a roll which can be served as is or enhanced with a cream or cheese sauce.

Canned salmon (red is best), drained, skin and round bones removed	2 × 7½ oz.	2 × 213 g
Finely chopped celery	½ cup	125 mL
Finely chopped onion	½ cup	125 mL
Egg	1	1
Lemon juice	¼ cup	50 mL
Salt	½ tsp.	2 mL
Pepper	⅛ tsp.	1 mL
All-purpose flour	2 cups	500 mL
Baking powder	4 tsp.	25 mL
Granulated sugar	2 tsp.	10 mL
Salt	½ tsp.	2 mL
Butter or margarine, cold	¼ cup	50 mL
Milk	¾ cup	175 mL

Mix first 7 ingredients together. Set aside.

Combine flour, baking powder, sugar and salt. Cut in butter until crumbly.

Add milk to flour mixture. Stir until ball forms. Turn out on lightly floured surface. Knead 8 times. Divide into 2 balls. Roll each ball into rectangle about 7 × 10 inches (18 × 25 cm). Spread with salmon mixture. Roll from long side as for jelly roll. Cut each roll into 8 slices. Lay cut side down on greased baking sheet. Bake in 400°F (200°C) oven for about 20 to 25 minutes until nicely browned. Makes 16.

Pictured on page 35.

Paré Pointer

You have seen everything when you see a salad bowl and a square dance.

TUNA STROGANOFF

Just the best flavor ever! Serve with rice or potatoes. Quick.

Chopped onion	1 cup	250 mL
Butter or margarine	2 tbsp.	30 mL
All-purpose flour	2 tbsp.	30 mL
Salt	½ tsp.	2 mL
Pepper	⅛ tsp.	0.5 mL
Sliced mushrooms, drained	10 oz.	284 mL
Condensed cream of mushroom soup	10 oz.	284 mL
Sour cream	½ cup	125 mL
Flaked tuna, drained	7 oz.	198 g

Sauté onion in butter in frying pan until soft and clear.

Mix in flour, salt, pepper and mushrooms.

Stir in mushroom soup until it boils and thickens.

Add sour cream and tuna. Stir. Heat through. Serves 4.

CRUMBED FISH SQUARES

Quick and easy to cook fish from the frozen state.

Frozen fish fillets	1 lb.	454 g
Egg	1	1
Water	1 tbsp.	15 mL
Fine dry bread crumbs	½ cup	125 mL
Salt	½ tsp.	2 mL
Pepper	⅛ tsp.	0.5 mL
Dill weed	1 tsp.	5 mL
Cooking oil		

Cut frozen fish as soon as you can. Let stand 5 to 10 minutes if necessary. Cut into 4 blocks to serve 2 and into 6 blocks to serve 3.

Beat egg and water together with fork.

Mix bread crumbs, salt, pepper and dill weed together.

Dip fish blocks into egg mixture then into crumbs. Fry in oil in frying pan until fish flakes easily when fork tested, about 7 minutes on each side. Serves 2 to 3.

SALMON LOAF

An old stand-by. Serve with or without sauce. Makes a small loaf.

Canned salmon, drained, skin and round bones removed	2 × 7½ oz.	2 × 213 g
Eggs, fork beaten	2	2
Dry bread crumbs	2 cups	450 mL
Finely chopped onion	½ cup	125 mL
Lemon juice	2 tbsp.	30 mL
Milk	½ cup	125 mL
Salt	¼ tsp.	1 mL
Dill weed	¼ tsp.	1 mL
DILL SAUCE		
Mayonnaise	½ cup	125 mL
Sour cream	¼ cup	60 mL
Lemon juice	2 tsp.	10 mL
Dill weed	1 tsp.	5 mL
Salt	¼ tsp.	1 mL

Mix first 8 ingredients together. Round bones of salmon may be added if mashed well. Pack into greased 8 × 4 inch (20 × 10 cm) loaf pan. Bake uncovered in 350°F (180°C) oven for 30 to 40 minutes. Serves 6.

Dill Sauce: Mix all ingredients together. Put a dollop on each slice of Salmon Loaf to serve.

Pictured on page 107.

ROLLED FISH FILLETS

Stuffed with shrimp, rolled fillets are easy to make. Cover with a lemon sauce for a dish with appeal.

Sole fillets (or other)	1 lb.	454 g
Broken shrimp, drained	4 oz.	113 g
Grated carrot	2 tbsp.	30 mL
Chopped green onion	2 tbsp.	30 mL
Salt, sprinkle		
Pepper, sprinkle		
Butter or margarine, melted	2 tbsp.	30 mL
Grated Cheddar cheese, for garnish		

(continued on next page)

Lay fillets on working surface.

Mash shrimp lightly. Divide and spread among fillets. Sprinkle with carrot, onion, salt and pepper. Roll. Place seam side down in greased baking pan.

Gently brush with melted butter. Bake uncovered in 425°F (220°C) oven for about 15 to 20 minutes until fish flakes easily when fork tested. Transfer to warmed platter. Spoon Lemon Sauce (page 42) over top.

Garnish with a bit of grated cheese. Serves 3 to 4.

Pictured on cover.

CRAB IMPERIAL

Good flavor with a golden meringue on top.

Green pepper, finely diced	1	1
Butter or margarine	3 tbsp.	50 mL
Chopped pimiento	2 tbsp.	30 mL
All-purpose flour	2 tbsp.	30 mL
Salt	1 tsp.	5 mL
Pepper	1/4 tsp.	1 mL
Milk	3/4 cup	175 mL
Mayonnaise	1/4 cup	50 mL
Dry mustard powder	1/2 tsp.	2 mL
Worcestershire sauce	1/4 tsp.	1 mL
Lemon juice	1 tsp.	5 mL
Egg yolks	3	3
Crabmeat	1 lb.	500 g
Egg whites, room temperature	3	3
Mayonnaise	2 tbsp.	30 mL

Sauté green pepper in butter until shrivelled.

Add pimiento, flour, salt and pepper. Mix. Stir in milk and first amount of mayonnaise until it boils and thickens. Remove from heat.

Stir in mustard, Worcestershire sauce, lemon juice and egg yolks. Fold in crabmeat. Spoon into 4 ramekins.

Beat egg whites until stiff. Fold in remaining mayonnaise. Spoon over ramekins. Bake in 350°F (180°C) oven for 15 to 20 minutes until golden and hot. Serves 4.

LOBSTER TAILS

An extra special treat. After you prepare one the rest will be easy. If using small sized lobster tails you may want to add steak to your menu.

Frozen uncooked lobster tails, thawed, 4 to 5 oz. (112 to 140 g) size	4	4
Butter or margarine (butter is best)		
Cayenne pepper		

Using kitchen shears, cut through shell down the center right to the end of shell only. If not completely thawed hold under room temperature tap water to hasten thawing. Spread shell apart slightly and cut meat down center being careful not to cut all the way through. Insert finger under meat (between meat and cartilage). Gently bring meat to top of shell. Push shell together so meat stays on top of shell.

Spread softened butter generously in a thick layer over meat. Sprinkle lightly with cayenne. Arrange on shallow baking pan. May be refrigerated at this point until ready to serve. Bake in 550°F (300°C) oven for about 7 minutes. Serve with melted butter in little bowls or dishes for dipping. Serves 4.

Pictured on page 17.

POACHED LOBSTER TAILS: Place thawed lobster tails in boiling salted water. Return to a boil. Cover and simmer for about 10 minutes. Remove cartilage and serve as is, or loosen and cut up meat and replace in shell before serving.

SOLE FULL OF SHRIMP

An easy way to stuff fillets. Curry powder gives a nice yellow color although you might like to try thyme as an alternative.

Cooked rice	1 cup	250 mL
Small or broken shrimp, drained	4 oz.	113 g
Salt	½ tsp.	2 mL
Curry powder (or thyme)	½ tsp.	2 mL
Butter or margarine, melted	¼ cup	60 mL
Sole fillets	1 lb.	454 g
Butter or margarine		

(continued on next page)

Mix rice, shrimp, salt, curry powder and first amount of butter together.

The easiest way to stuff the fish is to let frozen block of fish stand at room temperature until it can be cut into two layers, about 15 minutes. Spread shrimp mixture between layers in pan to fit. Dot with butter. Bake uncovered in 350°F (180°C) oven for about 30 minutes or until fish flakes easily when fork tested. Fillets may be laid out flat, stuffing put on top and then covered with rest of fillets. Serves 3 to 4.

TROUT STUFFED WITH SHRIMP: Stuff whole trout with filling.

CLAM PIE

An interesting way to serve clams. May be used as an appetizer as well as a main course.

Butter or margarine	¼ cup	60 mL
Chopped onion	1 cup	250 mL
All-purpose flour	1 tbsp.	15 mL
Salt	½ tsp.	2 mL
Pepper	⅛ tsp.	0.5 mL
Milk	1 cup	225 mL
Mashed potato	1 cup	225 mL
Minced clams (or baby clams), drain, reserve juice	2 × 5 oz.	2 × 142 g
Pastry, your own or a mix, see page 37		

Melt butter in frying pan. Add onion. Sauté until clear and soft.

Mix in flour, salt and pepper. Stir in milk until it boils and thickens.

Add potato. Mix. Stir in clams. Cool to lukewarm.

Roll pastry and line 9 inch (22 cm) pie plate. Put in clam filling adding some reserved juice if too thick. Smooth top. Roll top crust. Dampen edges with water. Put on top crust. Press to seal. Cut slits in top. Trim edges. Bake in 425°F (220°C) oven on lower shelf until browned, about 20 to 30 minutes. Serves 6.

Pictured on page 53.

SEAFOOD BAKE

A very good large recipe which can be halved. The addition of sour cream makes it softer and more mellow.

Cooked crabmeat	1 lb.	454 g
Cooked shrimp, deveined	1 lb.	454 g
Finely chopped onion	1 cup	250 mL
Finely chopped celery	1 cup	250 mL
Mayonnaise	1 cup	250 mL
Chopped green pepper	½ cup	125 mL
Worcestershire sauce	1 tbsp.	15 mL
Salt	½ tsp.	2 mL
Pepper	⅛ tsp.	0.5 mL
Sour cream (optional)	1 cup	250 mL
Dry bread crumbs	½ cup	125 mL
Butter or margarine, melted	2 tbsp.	30 mL

Mix first 10 ingredients together. Put into 3 quart (3 L) casserole.

Mix crumbs with melted butter. Spread over top. Bake uncovered in 350°F (180°C) oven for about 30 minutes. Serves 8.

Pictured on page 107.

SALMON CROQUETTES

No dipping or breading necessary. These are crusty good.

Salmon, drained, reserve juice	2 × 7½ oz.	2 × 213 g
Egg	1	1
Salt	½ tsp.	2 mL
Pepper	⅛ tsp.	0.5 mL
Worcestershire sauce	½ tsp.	2 mL
Reserved juice	¼ cup	60 mL
All-purpose flour	½ cup	125 mL
Baking powder	1 tbsp.	15 mL
Fat for deep-frying		

Combine first 6 ingredients in bowl. Mix well.

Add flour and baking powder. Stir together.

Drop by rounded spoonfuls into hot 375°F (180°C) fat. Brown completely. Makes 16 croquettes.

Pictured on page 71.

CRAB IN THE PINK

Prepare this in a saucepan. Ketchup adds color as well as flavor. Perfect served over rice.

Green onions, chopped	3	3
Butter or margarine	¼ cup	60 mL
All-purpose flour	2 tbsp.	30 mL
Salt	¼ tsp.	1 mL
Pepper	⅛ tsp.	0.5 mL
Light cream (or milk)	1 cup	225 mL
Ketchup	¼ cup	60 mL
Crabmeat	1 cup	250 mL
Worcestershire sauce	1 tsp.	5 mL

Sauté onion in butter in saucepan until soft.

Mix in flour, salt and pepper. Stir in cream and ketchup until it boils and thickens.

Add crabmeat and Worcestershire sauce. Stir. Heat through. Serves 2 to 3.

SPEEDY BAKED FISH

Pop frozen blocks into the oven with a colorful sauce. Nothing to it.

Frozen fish fillets	2 lbs.	2 × 454 g
Condensed cream of chicken soup	10 oz.	284 mL
Chopped onion	½ cup	125 mL
Lemon juice	2 tsp.	10 mL
Granulated sugar	½ tsp.	2 mL
Salt	½ tsp.	2 mL
Paprika	¼ tsp.	1 mL
Tomato, diced	1	1

Place frozen fish in ungreased small roaster or baking pan.

Mix remaining ingredients together. Pour over fish. Cover. Bake in 350°F (180°C) oven for 35 to 40 minutes until fish flakes easily when fork tested. Serves 4 to 6.

FINNAN HADDIE

This smoked and salted haddock is a member of the cod family. Very popular in Scotland.

Finnan Haddie, cut in serving size pieces	2 lbs.	900 g
Water to cover		
Butter or margarine	3 tbsp.	50 mL
All-purpose flour	3 tbsp.	50 mL
Salt	½ tsp.	2 mL
Pepper	⅛ tsp.	0.5 mL
Milk	1½ cups	350 mL
Parsley flakes (optional)	½ tsp.	2 mL

Put fish into saucepan and cover with water. Bring to a boil. Simmer slowly to poach until fish flakes easily when fork tested, about 5 to 8 minutes. Drain.

Melt butter in saucepan over medium heat. Mix in flour, salt and pepper. Stir in milk and parsley flakes until it boils and thickens. Cover fish with sauce in serving bowl. Serves 5 to 6.

SEAFOOD DUET

Shrimp and crab sauced, sprinkled with cheese and baked.

Condensed cream of celery soup	10 oz.	284 mL
Sliced mushrooms, drained	10 oz.	284 mL
Small cocktail shrimp, drained	4 oz.	113 g
Canned crab, cartilage removed	5 oz.	142 g
Egg	1	1
Dry bread crumbs	¼ cup	60 mL
Butter or margarine, melted	¼ cup	60 mL
Milk	¼ cup	60 mL
Grated medium Cheddar cheese	¼ cup	60 mL

Measure first 8 ingredients into bowl. Mix together. Turn into 1½ quart (1.5 L) casserole.

Sprinkle with grated cheese. Bake uncovered in 350°F (180°C) oven for 45 minutes. Serves 4.

JUST FOR THE HALIBUT

Grated Parmesan adds to the flavor of this crumbed and browned dish. The rich brown color comes from dry onion soup. Very good.

Dry onion soup	2 tbsp.	30 mL
Fine dry bread crumbs	1 cup	250 mL
Grated Parmesan cheese	2 tbsp.	30 mL
Parsley flakes	1 tsp.	5 mL
Salt	1 tsp.	5 mL
Pepper	1/4 tsp.	1 mL
Paprika	1/2 tsp.	2 mL
Halibut fillets	2 lbs.	2 × 454 g
Sour cream	1 cup	250 mL
Butter or margarine, melted	1/4 cup	60 mL

Mix first 7 ingredients together in small bowl.

Dip fish fillets into sour cream then into crumb mixture. Place on well greased shallow baking pan.

Drizzle with melted butter. Bake in 500°F (260°C) oven for 10 to 12 minutes until fish flakes easily when fork tested. Serves 4 to 6.

CHEEZY SALMON BAKE

Adding mushrooms and cheese to this loaf-type salmon raises it to a special level.

Canned salmon, with juice	2 × 7½ oz.	2 × 213 g
Eggs	2	2
Dry bread crumbs	1 cup	250 mL
Grated medium Cheddar cheese	1 cup	250 mL
Canned sliced mushrooms, drained	1/3 cup	75 mL
Lemon juice	1 tbsp.	15 mL
Worcestershire sauce	1/2 tsp.	2 mL
Onion salt	1/2 tsp.	2 mL

Remove skin and round bones from salmon. Round bones may be used if mashed well. Break up salmon.

In medium size bowl beat eggs until frothy. Mix in remaining ingredients. Add salmon and juice. Stir well. Turn into 1 quart (1 L) casserole. Bake uncovered in 350°F (180°C) oven for about 30 to 40 minutes. Serves 4.

TROUT AMANDINE

A beautiful golden color. A picture.

All-purpose flour	¼ cup	60 mL
Seasoned salt	1 tsp.	5 mL
Paprika	1 tsp.	5 mL
Margarine (butter browns too fast)	¼ cup	60 mL
Trout fillets, about ½ lb.	4	4
(250 g) each		
Butter or margarine	½ cup	125 mL
Sliced almonds	½ cup	125 mL
Lemon juice	1 tbsp.	15 mL

Mix flour, salt and paprika together.

Melt margarine in frying pan. Dip fish fillets into flour mixture. Brown both sides in margarine until golden brown.

Melt butter in saucepan or small frying pan. Add almonds. Heat and stir until nuts and butter brown, taking care not to burn butter.

Add lemon juice. Heat through. Place fish on warm serving platter or on individual plates. Spoon butter-nut mixture over top. Serves 4.

FISH CAKES

About the best way to use leftover fish. Stretches a small amount.

Cooked fish, boneless	1 cup	250 mL
Mashed potato	1 cup	250 mL
Finely chopped onion	¼ cup	60 mL
Salt	½ tsp.	2 mL
Pepper	⅛ tsp.	0.5 mL
Butter or margarine	2 tbsp.	30 mL

Flake fish. Add potato, onion, salt and pepper. Shape into patties.

Fry in butter turning to brown both sides. Makes 6 fish cakes to serve 2 or 3 people.

POACHED SALMON

You may prefer this plain or sauced. Eggs may be omitted if a plain cream sauce is desired.

Salmon chunk (tail section is good)	1½ lbs.	675 g
Salted water, to cover		
EGG SAUCE		
Butter or margarine	¼ cup	60 mL
All-purpose flour	¼ cup	60 mL
Salt	1 tsp.	5 mL
Pepper	¼ tsp.	1 mL
Milk	2 cups	450 mL
Chopped chives	1 tsp.	5 mL
Hard-boiled eggs, chopped	2	2

Poach fish in simmering salted water until it flakes easily when fork tested, about 15 to 20 minutes. Remove skin and bones. Break into pieces. Put into serving bowl. Keep hot. Pour Egg Sauce over top. Serves 4.

Egg Sauce: Melt butter in saucepan over medium heat. Mix in flour, salt and pepper. Stir in milk until it boils and thickens.

Add chives and eggs. Simmer gently to heat and soften chives. Pour over cooked fish. Makes 2 cups (450 mL).

TUNA PORCUPINES

Aptly named, these are a result of stretching a can of tuna with rice.

Flaked tuna, drained	7 oz.	198 g
Long grain rice	½ cup	125 mL
Chopped onion	½ cup	125 mL
Salt	½ tsp.	2 mL
Pepper	⅛ tsp.	0.5 mL
Egg, fork beaten	1	1
Condensed cream of mushroom soup	10 oz.	284 mL
Water	⅔ cup	150 mL

Mix first 6 ingredients together in bowl. Shape into about 14 balls. Place in 9 × 9 inch (22 × 22 cm) greased baking dish.

Stir soup and water together well. Pour over balls. Cover. Bake in 350°F (180°C) oven for 1 hour until rice is cooked. Serves 4.

Pictured on page 71.

TROUT HOLLANDAISE

Top these beauties with a shrimp and mushroom sauce.

Trout, about ½ lb. (250 g) each, head and tail removed	4	4
Water	½ cup	125 mL
Cooking oil	2 tbsp.	30 mL
Salt, sprinkle		
Pepper, sprinkle		
HOLLANDAISE SAUCE		
Egg yolks	3	3
Butter or margarine, melted	1 cup	250 mL
Lemon juice	1 tbsp.	15 mL
Chopped cooked shrimp	1 cup	250 mL
Finely chopped fresh mushrooms	½ cup	125 mL
Paprika	¼ tsp.	1 mL
Salt	¼ tsp.	1 mL
Pepper	⅛ tsp.	0.5 mL

Arrange trout in baking pan. Add water and cooking oil. Sprinkle with salt and pepper. Bake covered in 450°F (230°C) oven for about 15 minutes, until it flakes easily when fork tested.

Hollandaise Sauce: Meanwhile put 3 egg yolks into top of double boiler over hot, not boiling, water. Stir. Add melted butter very slowly, stirring continuously until thickened. Add lemon juice. Stir.

Add shrimp and mushrooms to sauce. Add paprika, salt and pepper. Heat through. Place fish on warm platter. Spoon sauce over top. Serves 4.

SALMON TOMATO FILLETS

A change of pace and taste. Good for any catch.

Salmon fillets (or steaks)	4	4
Canned tomatoes	14 oz.	398 mL
Chopped onion	1 cup	250 mL
Granulated sugar	1 tsp.	5 mL
Parsley flakes	1 tsp.	5 mL
Salt	1 tsp.	5 mL
Pepper	⅛ tsp.	0.5 mL

(continued on next page)

Arrange fillets in baking pan large enough to hold in single layer.

Measure remaining ingredients into saucepan. Bring to a boil while stirring and simmer for 10 minutes. Pour over fish. Bake uncovered in 350°F (180°C) oven until fish flakes easily when fork tested, about 15 to 20 minutes. Serves 4.

HALIBUT STEAK

A good way to dress up fish. Sauced and cheezed.

Halibut steaks or fillets (or other fish)	**4**	**4**
Salt, sprinkle		
Pepper, sprinkle		
Butter or margarine	**¼ cup**	**60 mL**
All-purpose flour	**¼ cup**	**60 mL**
Salt	**1 tsp.**	**5 mL**
Pepper	**¼ tsp.**	**1 mL**
Cayenne pepper	**⅛ tsp.**	**0.5 mL**
Milk	**2 cups**	**450 mL**
Grated medium Cheddar cheese	**½ cup**	**125 mL**

Place fish in single layer in baking pan. Sprinkle with first amount of salt and pepper.

Melt butter in saucepan. Mix in flour, remaining salt and pepper and cayenne pepper. Stir in milk until it boils and thickens. Spoon sauce over fish.

Sprinkle with cheese. Add more if desired. Bake uncovered in 350°F (180°C) oven for about 25 minutes until fish flakes easily when fork tested. Serves 4.

HALIBUT WITH ONION: Pan fry fish with sliced onion in cooking oil, about 5 minutes per side. If you have never fried onion with fish be sure to try this. Very good.

Paré Pointer

Rabbits don't like combs. They prefer hare brushes.

TUNA SCALLOP

Another good dish built on economy with an added bonus of good taste as well.

Butter or margarine	¼ cup	60 mL
All-purpose flour	¼ cup	60 mL
Salt	1 tsp.	5 mL
Pepper	¼ tsp.	1 mL
Granulated sugar	1 tsp.	5 mL
Milk	2 cups	450 mL
Eggs, beaten	2	2
Onion flakes	1 tbsp.	15 mL
Flaked tuna, drained	7 oz.	198 mL
Parsley flakes	½ tsp.	2 mL
Lemon juice	1 tbsp.	15 mL
Chopped pimiento	1 tbsp.	15 mL
Dry bread crumbs	½ cup	125 mL
Butter or margarine, melted	2 tbsp.	30 mL

Melt butter in saucepan over medium heat. Stir in flour, salt, pepper and sugar. Stir in milk until it boils and thickens. Remove from heat.

Stir in eggs. Stir in onion flakes, tuna, parsley, lemon juice and pimiento. Turn into 1 quart (1 L) casserole.

Mix bread crumbs with melted butter. Sprinkle over casserole. Bake uncovered in 350°F (180°C) oven for 40 to 45 minutes. Serves 4.

1. Salmon Rolls page 20
2. Orange Spareribs page 111
3. Curried Ham Rolls page 93

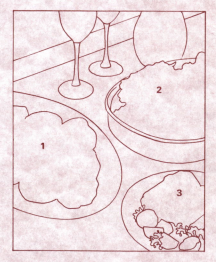

BAKED SALMON STEAKS

Baking these takes the work out of cooking.

Salmon steaks, cut 1 inch (2.5 cm) thick	4	4
Salt, sprinkle		
Pepper, sprinkle		
Sour cream	½ cup	125 mL
Dry onion flakes, crushed	1 tsp.	5 mL
Tarragon (or dill weed)	½ tsp.	2 mL

Arrange salmon steaks in baking pan large enough to hold in single layer. Sprinkle with salt and pepper.

Mix sour cream, onion flakes and tarragon together. Spread over salmon. Bake uncovered in 450°F (230°C) oven until fish flakes easily when fork tested, about 15 to 20 minutes. Serves 4.

PIE CRUST PASTRY

For meat in pastry dishes.

All-purpose flour	5 cups	1.1 L
Salt	2 tsp.	10 mL
Baking powder	1 tsp.	5 mL
Brown sugar	3 tbsp.	50 mL
Lard, room temperature	1 lb.	454 g
Egg	1	1
Vinegar	2 tbsp.	30 mL
Add cold water, to make	1 cup	225 mL

Measure flour, salt, baking powder and brown sugar into large bowl. Stir together to distribute all ingredients.

Add lard. Cut into pieces with knife. With pastry cutter, cut in lard until whole mixture is crumbly and feels moist.

Break egg into measuring cup. Fork beat well. Add vinegar. Add cold water to measure 1 cup (225 mL). Pour slowly over flour mixture stirring with fork to distribute. With hands, work until it will hold together. Divide into 4 equal parts. Each part is sufficient for an 8 to 9 inch (20 to 22 cm) 2-crust pie. Use now or wrap in plastic and store in refrigerator for 1 or 2 weeks. Store in freezer to have a continuing supply.

LOADED BISCUITS

Full flavored biscuits to round out any meal. Quick and easy.

All-purpose flour	2 cups	450 mL
Granulated sugar	2 tbsp.	30 mL
Baking powder	4 tsp.	20 mL
Salt	1 tsp.	5 mL
Grated sharp Cheddar cheese (Imperial is good)	1¼ cups	300 mL
Finely chopped green onion	3 tbsp.	50 mL
Finely chopped green pepper	2 tbsp.	30 mL
Cooking oil	⅓ cup	75 mL
Cold milk	¾ cup	175 mL

Measure flour, sugar, baking powder and salt into mixing bowl. Stir well. Add cheese, onion and green pepper. Stir lightly to mix.

Add cooking oil and milk. Stir to mix into a soft ball. Turn out onto lightly floured surface. Knead 8 to 10 times. Roll or pat to ¾ inch (2 cm) thickness. Cut with 2¼ inch (5 cm) round floured cookie cutter. Arrange on ungreased baking sheet. Bake in 425°F (210°C) oven for about 15 minutes until browned. Makes 12.

Pictured on page 125.

STUFFING BALLS

An ideal way to serve individual stuffing, especially with poultry that isn't roasted. Good served with roast veal, pork and ham.

Butter or margarine	¼ cup	60 mL
Chopped onion	½ cup	125 mL
Chopped celery	½ cup	125 mL
Cream style corn	14 oz.	398 mL
Water	½ cup	125 mL
Poultry seasoning	1½ tsp.	7 mL
Salt	1 tsp.	5 mL
Pepper	¼ tsp.	1 mL
Parsley flakes	2 tsp.	10 mL
Course bread crumbs	6 cups	1.35 L
Eggs, fork beaten	3	3
Butter or margarine, melted	½ cup	125 mL

(continued on next page)

Melt butter in frying pan. Add onion and celery. Sauté until tender.

Add corn, water, poultry seasoning, salt, pepper and parsley flakes. Stir. Bring to a boil.

Put bread crumbs into bowl. Pour hot corn mixture over top. Mix together.

Add eggs. Mix well. Shape into balls. An ice cream scoop ensures fast, even sizing. Put into small roaster or baking dish in single layer.

Pour butter over balls. Cover. Bake in 350°F (180°C) oven for about 25 minutes. These may be refrigerated overnight before baking. Makes 18 stuffing balls.

Pictured on page 143.

HUSH PUPPIES

Long ago in the southeastern United States the wives of fishermen used these to quiet their barking dogs. They are still served with seafood in that area.

White or yellow cornmeal	1½ cups	350 mL
Water	1½ cups	350 mL
Milk	⅓ cup	75 mL
Very finely chopped onion	⅓ cup	75 mL
Eggs, beaten	2	2
Cooking oil	1 tbsp.	15 mL
All-purpose flour	1 cup	225 mL
Baking powder	1 tbsp.	15 mL
Salt	2 tsp.	10 mL
Granulated sugar	2 tsp.	10 mL
Fat for deep-frying		

Heat cornmeal and water in medium size saucepan until fairly stiff. Remove from heat.

Add milk and onion. Mix well. Add beaten eggs and cooking oil. Stir.

Add next 4 ingredients. Mix together.

Drop by rounded teaspoonfuls into hot fat 375°F (190°C) until browned. Turn to brown evenly. Makes 4 dozen.

CUCUMBER SAUCE

Good with any fish but especially with Seafood Wellington, see page 9.

Sour cream	½ cup	125 mL
Mayonnaise	¼ cup	60 mL
Chives	2 tsp.	10 mL
Parsley flakes	2 tsp.	10 mL
Lemon juice	1 tsp.	5 mL
Salt	¼ tsp.	1 mL
Onion powder	¼ tsp.	1 mL
Medium cucumber, with skin, halved lengthwise, seeded and grated	1	1

Mix first 7 ingredients together. Chill.

Once cucumber is grated, drain thoroughly. Add to sour cream mixture shortly before serving so it doesn't cause sauce to go watery. Place a large dollop of sauce on each dinner plate with Seafood Wellington. Makes about 1⅓ cups (300 mL).

POPOVERS

These are put into a cold oven and then the heat is turned on. It works.

Eggs	4	4
Milk	1½ cups	350 mL
All-purpose flour	1½ cups	350 mL
Salt	1 tsp.	2 mL
Butter or margarine, melted	1 tbsp.	15 mL

Beat eggs in bowl. Mix in milk. Beat in flour and salt until bubbly. Add melted butter. Pour into well greased muffin tins about ½ full. Place in cold oven. Turn temperature to 400°F (200°C). Bake for about 40 minutes until puffed and well browned. Makes 12.

YORKSHIRE PUDDING: Omit melted butter. Pour ¼ cup (60 mL) hot drippings from roast into 8 × 8 inch (20 × 20 cm) pan. Pour in batter. Bake uncovered in 425°F (220°C) oven until risen and browned, about 30 minutes. Cut into squares to serve.

BLUE CHEESE SAUCE

Mellow with a fairly mild cheese flavor. Add more freely to taste.

Sour cream	1 cup	250 mL
Cream cheese, softened	4 oz.	125 g
Blue cheese, crumbled	3 tbsp.	50 mL
Onion salt	¼ tsp.	1 mL

Combine all ingredients in bowl. Beat until very well mixed. Chill. Serve with any fish, especially Tuna Ring (page 14). Try putting a dollop on steak. Makes about 1½ cups (375 mL).

Pictured on page 89.

SEAFOOD SAUCE

Just the sauce for deep-fried seafood.

Ketchup	¾ cup	175 mL
Horseradish	2 tsp.	10 mL
Sweet pickle relish	3 tbsp.	50 mL
Vinegar	1 tbsp.	15 mL
Dry onion flakes, crushed	1 tsp.	5 mL
Worcestershire sauce	1 tsp.	5 mL

Mix all ingredients together. Chill until needed. Makes about 1 cup (250 mL) sauce.

TARTAR SAUCE

No fish is complete without it.

Mayonnaise	1 cup	250 mL
Chopped dill pickle	¼ cup	60 mL
(or sweet pickle relish)		
Lemon juice	1 tbsp.	15 mL
Chopped pimiento	1 tsp.	5 mL
(or stuffed olives)		
Parsley flakes	1 tsp.	5 mL
Onion powder	⅛ tsp.	0.5 mL

Mix all ingredients together. Chill until needed. Makes 1 cup (250 mL).

LEMON SAUCE

A perfect sauce for fish.

Butter or margarine	2 tbsp.	30 mL
All-purpose flour	2 tbsp.	30 mL
Salt	1/2 tsp.	2 mL
Pepper (white is best), light sprinkle		
Onion powder	1/8 tsp.	0.5 mL
Milk	1 cup	225 mL
Lemon juice	2 tbsp.	30 mL
Butter or margarine (optional)	2 tbsp.	30 mL
Egg (optional)	1	1

Melt first amount of butter in small saucepan. Mix in flour, salt, pepper and onion powder.

Add milk and lemon juice. Heat and stir until it boils and thickens. May be served now or add remaining ingredients.

Put sauce into blender. Add second amount of butter and egg. Blend until smooth. Return to saucepan. Heat and whisk until it starts to boil. If sauce curdles run through blender. Serve over fish, seafood or poultry. Makes 1 1/2 cups (350 mL).

MUSTARD SAUCE

A must to serve with a ham loaf or patties. Terrific condiment.

Chopped onion	1/3 cup	75 mL
Butter or margarine	2 tbsp.	30 mL
All-purpose flour	1 tbsp.	15 mL
Salt	1/4 tsp.	1 mL
Milk	1 cup	250 mL
Prepared mustard	1 tbsp.	15 mL
Lemon juice	1 tbsp.	15 mL

Sauté onion in butter in saucepan until soft.

Mix in flour and salt.

Add milk, mustard and lemon juice. Stir until it boils and thickens. Serve with corned beef, ham or any other meat. Makes 1 cup (250 mL).

HORSERADISH SAUCE

Makes a fluffy light sauce and also stretches the horseradish. Makes it milder too.

Sour cream	½ cup	125 mL
Horseradish	½ cup	125 mL
Mayonnaise	3 tbsp.	50 mL

Mix all ingredients together. Chill until needed. Makes a generous 1 cup (250 mL).

Variation: Mix in ¼ tsp. (1 mL) curry powder.

STEAK ROLL

Steak is stuffed with mushrooms, Parmesan cheese and onion. Has a very tasty gravy.

Fresh mushrooms	1 lb.	450 g
Chopped onion	½ cup	125 mL
Grated Parmesan cheese	1 cup	250 mL
Dry bread crumbs	¼ cup	60 mL
Salt	1 tsp.	5 mL
Pepper	¼ tsp.	1 mL
Round steak	2 lbs.	900 g
Margarine (butter browns too fast)	2 tbsp.	30 mL
Mushroom caps		
Beef bouillon cubes	2 × ⅕ oz.	2 × 6 g
Boiling water	1⅔ cups	400 mL

Remove stems from mushrooms. Set caps aside. Chop stems. Combine stems, onion, cheese, crumbs, salt and pepper in bowl.

Lay steak on working surface. Pound thin. Spread cheese mixture over top. Roll. Tie with string. Brown extra well in margarine in frying pan. Put into small roaster.

Put mushroom caps in roaster. Dissolve beef cubes in boiling water. Pour over meat and mushroom caps. Cover. Bake in 350°F (180°C) oven for 1½ to 2 hours until tender. Serve in slices. Serves 4 to 6.

Note: To thicken sauce, mix 2 tbsp. (30 mL) all-purpose flour with 4 tbsp. (60 mL) water until smooth for each 1 cup (250 mL) sauce. Boil and stir to thicken.

SWISS STEAK AND TOMATOES

Fix it and forget it. It cooks in a tomato gravy.

Round steak	2 lbs.	900 g
All-purpose flour	1/3 cup	75 mL
Salt	1 1/2 tsp.	7 mL
Pepper	1/4 tsp.	1 mL
Cooking oil	3 tbsp.	50 mL
Medium onions, sliced or chopped	2	2
Stewed tomatoes, mashed	14 oz.	398 mL
Green pepper, cut in strips	1	1
Garlic powder	1/4 tsp.	1 mL
Apple juice	1/2 cup	125 mL
Red wine vinegar	4 tsp.	20 mL
Beef bouillon cubes	3 × 1/5 oz.	3 × 6 g
Boiling water	2 1/2 cups	600 mL

Cut meat into serving size pieces.

Mix flour, salt and pepper together.

Dip meat into flour mixture. Brown in hot oil in frying pan. Put into small roaster.

Sauté onion until soft, adding more oil if needed. Add to meat.

Add tomatoes, green pepper, garlic powder, apple juice and vinegar.

Dissolve beef cubes in water. Add. Stir lightly. Cover. Bake in 350°F (180°C) oven until tender, about 1 1/2 hours. Serves 6.

SALISBURY STEAK

This steak is actually a meat patty which anyone can eat with ease.

Lean ground beef	1 1/2 lbs.	700 g
Cooking oil	2 tbsp.	30 mL
Salt, sprinkle		
Pepper, sprinkle		
Large onion, thinly sliced in rings	1	1
Water (or more if needed)	1/3 cup	75 mL

(continued on next page)

Shape meat into 4 patties 6 oz. (168 g) each. Brown in cooking oil in frying pan. Sprinkle with salt and pepper after turning. Continue to cook until desired stage of doneness.

Add onion to pan if there is room or use another frying pan adding a bit of cooking oil. Sauté until soft and browned.

To serve put steaks on warm plates or platter. Divide onion rings over top. Stir water into pan removing all crusty bits. A bit of Worcestershire sauce or beef bouillon powder may be added if juice hasn't enough flavor. Spoon over all. Serves 4.

MOCK DUCK

Mock Duck is round steak or flank rolled around stuffing.

Dry bread crumbs	1¼ cups	275 mL
Dry onion flakes	2 tbsp.	30 mL
Celery flakes	1 tsp.	5 mL
Poultry seasoning	1 tsp.	5 mL
Parsley flakes	1 tsp.	5 mL
Salt	½ tsp.	2 mL
Pepper	⅛ tsp.	0.5 mL
Butter or margarine, melted	2 tbsp.	30 mL
Water (more or less)	6 tbsp.	100 mL
Complete round of steak, ½ to ¾ inch (12 to 18 mm) thick	2 lbs.	900 g
Salt, sprinkle		
Butter or margarine, melted	2 tbsp.	30 mL
Water	1 cup	250 mL

Mix first 7 ingredients together in bowl.

Stir in first amount of melted butter. Add first amount of water, just enough to dampen so mixture will hold together when squeezed.

Lay out round of steak. Sprinkle with salt. Spread with stuffing not quite to edges. Roll. Tie with string. Place in small roaster.

Pour remaining melted butter over top. Add remaining water to roaster. Cover. Roast in 325°F (160°C) oven until tender, about 2 to 3 hours. Check halfway through cooking to see if it is dry. Add more water if needed. Serves 4 to 6.

BEEF BOURGUIGNON

Serve this well known dish complete with gravy. Alcohol-free red wine may be used if preferred for a genuine flavor.

Boneless lean beef, chuck or rump steak	2 lbs.	900 g
Butter or margarine	2 tbsp.	30 mL
Cooking oil	2 tbsp.	30 mL
Small fresh mushrooms	½ lb.	225 g
All-purpose flour	¼ cup	60 mL
Salt	½ tsp.	2 mL
Pepper	½ tsp.	2 mL
Burgundy (or alcohol-free red wine)	2 cups	500 mL
Garlic powder (or 1 clove, minced)	¼ tsp.	1 mL
Bay leaf	1	1
Ketchup	1 tbsp.	15 mL
Parsley flakes	1 tsp.	5 mL
Thyme	½ tsp.	2 mL
Beef bouillon cubes	3 × ⅕ oz.	3 × 6 g
Boiling water	1 cup	250 mL
Canned small onions, drained (see Note)	14 oz.	398 mL

Cut beef into 1 inch (2.5 cm) cubes. Brown in butter and cooking oil in frying pan. Transfer to large saucepan when browned.

Sauté mushrooms in frying pan for 3 to 4 minutes. Add to meat in saucepan.

Put flour, salt and pepper into frying pan. Add enough butter or margarine to moisten flour if needed. Stir in Burgundy, garlic powder, bay leaf, ketchup, parsley flakes and thyme until it boils and thickens.

Dissolve beef cubes in boiling water. Add to wine mixture. Stir. Pour over meat. Cover. Simmer for 1 hour.

Add onions. Simmer, covered, for about 30 minutes more until tender. Discard bay leaf. Serves 6.

Note: If you cannot find canned onions, substitute 1½ cups (375 mL) cooked whole pearl onions or cut-up onions, cooked.

Paré Pointer

No dear, you don't charge batteries with a credit card.

BEEF BURGUNDY

A simple European dish. Full flavored.

Beef sirloin, cubed	1 lb.	454 g
Margarine (butter browns too fast)	2 tbsp.	30 mL
Fresh mushrooms, sliced	1 cup	250 mL
Green onions, sliced	3	3
All-purpose flour	1 tsp.	5 mL
Burgundy (or alcohol-free red wine)	²/₃ cup	150 mL
Water	½ cup	125 mL
Salt	½ tsp.	2 mL

Brown meat in margarine in frying pan. Transfer to saucepan.

Brown mushrooms and onion in frying pan.

Mix in flour. Add Burgundy, water and salt. Stir until it boils. Pour over meat. Cover. Simmer until tender when pierced with fork, about 40 to 60 minutes. Serves 2.

FOILED STEAK

So tender even though a less tender steak is used. Nice reddish color.

Chuck or blade steak, cut in serving size pieces	2 lbs.	900 g
Envelope dry onion soup	1	1
Sliced mushrooms, drained	10 oz.	284 mL
Canned tomatoes, drained, reserve juice	19 oz.	540 mL
Juice from tomatoes	½ cup	125 mL
Cornstarch	1 tbsp.	15 mL
Ketchup	1 tbsp.	15 mL
Worcestershire sauce	1 tsp.	5 mL

Place large piece of foil on baking sheet or in roaster. Arrange meat on foil. Sprinkle with soup, mushrooms and cut up tomatoes.

Mix juice and cornstarch together in small saucepan over low heat. Add ketchup and Worcestershire sauce. Stir until it boils and thickens. Pour over all. Seal foil tightly. Bake in 300°F (150°C) oven for about 2½ hours until tender. Serves 6.

MEATBALL STEW

A good use for hamburger. No pre-browning needed.

MEATBALLS

Ground beef	1 lb.	450 g
Dry bread crumbs (or rolled oats)	½ cup	125 mL
Ketchup	2 tbsp.	30 mL
Salt	1 tsp.	5 mL
Pepper	¼ tsp.	1 mL
Egg, fork beaten	1	1

SAUCE

Beef bouillon cubes	4 × ⅕ oz.	4 × 6 g
Boiling water	2 cups	450 mL
Water	2 cups	450 mL
Celery ribs, sliced	4	4
Medium onions, cut in eighths	2	2
Medium carrots, cut in sticks	6	6
Medium potatoes, cut bite size	4 - 6	4 - 6
Thyme (optional)	⅛ tsp.	0.5 mL

Meatballs: Mix all ingredients together. Shape into 24 balls. Set aside.

Sauce: Dissolve beef cubes in boiling water in large saucepan. Add remaining water. Drop in meatballs. Bring to a boil. Cover and simmer gently for 15 minutes.

Add remaining ingredients. Return to a boil. Cover. Simmer 15 minutes more or until vegetables are cooked. Add more water if needed. If desired, thicken juice. Mix 1 tbsp. (15 mL) flour and 2 tbsp. (30 mL) water for each 1 cup (250 mL) juice. Mix until smooth. Stir into boiling juice to thicken. Serves 4.

STANDING RIB ROAST

King of roasts, this cut is tender enough to be cooked without a cover if you wish.

Rib roast	4½ lbs.	2 kg
Salt, sprinkle		
Pepper, sprinkle		

(continued on next page)

Place meat fat side up in roaster. Sprinkle with salt and pepper. Cover or not as you please. Roast in 325°F (160°C) oven about 3 hours for well done. Cover may be removed to brown during last few minutes. If rare to medium-rare is desired, it would be better to cook uncovered. A thermometer is best for this roast unless it is to be well done. Remove cooked roast to platter. Keep warm while making gravy. Serve with Horseradish Sauce (page 43). Serves 6.

GRAVY

Beef fat	½ cup	125 mL
All-purpose flour	½ cup	125 mL
Salt	1 tsp.	5 mL
Pepper	¼ tsp.	1 mL
Drippings plus water to equal	4 cups	1L

Use measured amount of fat. If necessary add butter or margarine. Mix in flour, salt and pepper. Whisk in drippings and water until it boils and thickens. Add a bit of gravy browner if too light in color. Taste for salt adding more if needed. Makes 4 cups (1L).

RIB EYE ROAST: Cook as above.

BONED AND ROLLED RIB ROAST: Cook as above.

LONDON BROIL

This flank steak has a very good flavorful marinade.

Flank steak	1½ lbs.	675 g
Cooking oil	1 tbsp.	15 mL
Vinegar	1 tbsp.	15 mL
Salt	1 tsp.	5 mL
Parsley flakes	1 tsp.	5 mL
Garlic powder	¼ tsp.	1 mL
Pepper	¼ tsp.	1 mL

Score meat in diamond shape pattern on both sides.

Mix remaining ingredients together in shallow pan. Add meat. Cover. Chill at least 2 hours turning often. Broil about 4 inches (10 cm) from heat for about 5 minutes on each side for rare meat. Placing knife almost flat on top of steak slice diagonally in very thin slices. Put each serving in a pile on each plate or pile all meat onto warmed plate or carve at the table. Serves 4 to 5.

PEPPER STEAK

Also known as Steak Au Poivre, this is really easy to make. Don't worry about the peppercorns. This is a bit peppery but not what you would expect. Very similar to a pricey restaurant's.

Black peppercorns	2 tbsp.	30 mL
Fillets or top grade steaks	4	4
Margarine (butter browns too fast)	2 tbsp.	30 mL
Cooking oil	2 tbsp.	30 mL
Chopped green onion	2 tbsp.	30 mL
Beef bouillon cube	1 × ⅕ oz.	1 × 6 g
Boiling water	½ cup	125 mL
Brandy (optional)	2 tbsp.	30 mL
Cornstarch	1 tsp.	5 mL
Water	1 tsp.	5 mL
Heavy cream	¼ cup	60 mL
Butter or margarine	2 tbsp.	30 mL

Crush peppercorns with mortar and pestle or place in plastic bag and pound with meat mallet or a hammer. Use heel of hand to push crushed peppercorns into meat on both sides. Cover and chill for 1 hour or more.

Heat margarine and cooking oil in frying pan. Brown steaks on both sides, cooking to desired degree of doneness. Transfer to baking dish and keep hot in oven.

Sauté onion in frying pan until soft adding more margarine if needed.

Dissolve bouillon cube in boiling water. Set aside.

Drain any excess fat from frying pan. Pour brandy into pan and ignite.

When flame dies add beef bouillon. Mix cornstarch with water and stir into bouillon to boil and thicken.

Stir in cream and butter. Heat through. If sauce is too thin, boil until reduced to consistency desired. Spoon over steak. Serves 4.

Sign in a local store — "Back in twenty minutes. Gone ten already."

PEKING ROAST

When you wish you could cook something in a completely different way, this is for you. Great served in cold sandwiches or for a lunch.

Beef roast, less tender cut	3 lbs.	1.35 kg
Cooking oil or margarine	2 tbsp.	30 mL
Prepared strong coffee	2 cups	500 mL
Chopped onion	½ cup	125 mL
Salt	1 tsp.	5 mL
Garlic powder	½ tsp.	2 mL
Pepper	¼ tsp.	1 mL

Brown meat well in hot oil in large heavy saucepan or Dutch oven over medium heat.

Add remaining ingredients. Bring to a boil. Cover. Simmer gently for about 3 hours until tender. Turn 2 or 3 times. The outside has an elusive flavor quite similar to a burned coffee taste. Since the flavor doesn't penetrate the meat very deeply, serve with juice served on the side or spooned over meat slices. Serves 6.

OVEN POT ROAST

All zipped up with a great gravy when finished. Let the oven do the work.

Beef roast, economy cut	3 lbs.	1.35 kg
Condensed cream of mushroom soup	10 oz.	284 mL
Envelope dry onion soup	1	1
Chopped onion	1 cup	250 mL
Water	1 cup	250 mL
Apple juice	½ cup	125 mL
Red wine vinegar	1 tbsp.	15 mL
Bay leaf	1	1
Thyme	½ tsp.	2 mL
Garlic powder	½ tsp.	2 mL

Place meat in roaster. For fat-free gravy trim fat.

Mix remaining ingredients together in bowl. Pour over meat. Cover. Bake in 325°F (160°C) oven until tender, about 3½ to 4 hours. Serves 6 if bone content is small.

ROUND STEAK ROAST

Covered with an onion and mushroom mixture, this steak is rolled then baked in apple juice and red vinegar. Good and different.

Round steak	2 lbs.	900 g
Onion, thinly sliced	1	1
Dry bread crumbs	½ cup	125 mL
Chopped fresh mushrooms	1½ cups	375 mL
Salt, good sprinkle		
Pepper, sprinkle		
Paprika, good sprinkle		
Egg	1	1
Water	1 tbsp.	15 mL
Apple juice	1¼ cups	300 mL
Red wine vinegar	3 tbsp.	50 mL

Leave steak whole. Pound thin.

Put onion over steak followed by crumbs, mushrooms, salt, pepper and paprika.

Beat egg with water. Drizzle over top. Roll up and tie with string. Put into small roaster.

Mix apple juice with vinegar. Pour over steak roll. Cover. Bake in 350°F (180°C) oven for 1½ to 2 hours until tender. Slice and place on warm platter. Serves 4 to 6.

1. Frankfurter Stew page 114
2. Chicken Cacciatore page 133
3. Clam Pie page 25

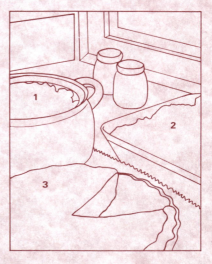

SAUCE BAKED MEATBALLS

The ultimate in flavor for a meatball. The liquid smoke adds to it. Add more to taste if you like. Even without any, these are great. No pre-browning required.

Egg	1	1
Milk or water	½ cup	125 mL
Rolled oats	1 cup	250 mL
Chopped onion	½ cup	125 mL
Salt	1 tsp.	5 mL
Pepper	¼ tsp.	1 mL
Garlic powder	¼ tsp.	1 mL
Chili powder	1 tsp.	5 mL
Ground beef	1½ lbs.	675 g
Ketchup	¾ cup	175 mL
Brown sugar	¾ cup	175 mL
Liquid smoke (optional)	2 tsp.	10 mL
Garlic powder	¼ tsp.	1 mL
Worcestershire sauce	1 tsp.	5 mL

Beat egg with spoon in bowl. Add next 8 ingredients. Mix thoroughly. Shape into meatballs the size of a walnut. Place in pan large enough to hold in single layer.

Combine remaining ingredients. Pour over meatballs. Bake covered in 350°F (180°C) oven for 1 hour. Serves 4 to 5.

JIFFY POT ROAST

Simply put this in the oven and forget it for the afternoon. It forms a super gravy which may be thickened if desired.

Beef roast, economy cut	4 lbs.	1.8 kg
Envelope dry onion soup	1	1
Condensed cream of mushroom soup	10 oz.	284 mL
Water	1 cup	250 mL

Place meat in roaster.

Mix both soups with water. Pour over meat. Cover roaster. Bake in 325°F (160°C) oven until tender, about 4 hours. For smaller roast use only ½ envelope dry soup. Serves 6 to 8 depending on bone content.

ROUND STEAK SUPREME

Dry onion soup and sour cream combine to make a very tasty meat. More cream and milk can be added to make more gravy if desired.

Round steak, cut in ¼ inch (6 mm) strips	1 lb.	500 g
Cooking oil	2 tbsp.	30 mL
Butter or margarine	1 tbsp.	15 mL
All-purpose flour	3 tbsp.	50 mL
Sour cream	1 cup	250 mL
Envelope dry onion soup	1	1
Whole or sliced mushrooms, drained	10 oz.	284 mL
Milk	½ cup	125 mL

Brown meat in cooking oil and butter.

Mix in flour. Stir in sour cream until it boils and thickens. Add onion soup, mushrooms and milk. Turn into 1 quart (1 L) casserole. Cover. Bake in 325°F (160°C) oven for 1 hour or so, until tender. This can also be simmered on top of the stove for about 30 minutes. Stir often and add more sour cream and milk if needed. Serves 2.

LIVER STROGANOFF

Sautéed liver in a stroganoff sauce with onion and mushrooms.

Baby beef liver, cut in 2½ inch (6.5 cm) strips	1 lb.	500 g
All-purpose flour, to coat		
Margarine (butter browns too fast)	2 tbsp.	30 mL
Margarine (butter browns too fast)	2 tbsp.	30 mL
Sliced mushrooms, drained	10 oz.	284 mL
Chopped onion	⅔ cup	150 mL
Condensed cream of mushroom soup	10 oz.	284 mL
Water	1 cup	250 mL
Worcestershire sauce	1 tsp.	5 mL
Salt	½ tsp.	2 mL
Pepper	⅛ tsp.	0.5 mL
Sour cream	1 cup	250 mL

(continued on next page)

Dredge liver in flour and brown in first amount of margarine in frying pan. When cooked, inside of the meat should change color to grey. Remove from pan.

Melt remaining margarine in pan. Add mushrooms and onion. Sauté until onion is soft.

Add soup, water, Worcestershire sauce, salt and pepper. Stir. Heat through. Stir in liver. Simmer for 7 to 8 minutes.

Add sour cream. Heat through. Serves 6.

CURRIED LIVER: Mix in a light sprinkle of curry powder. Stir and taste. Add more as desired. Now, this is excellent!

STEWED MEATBALLS

No need to brown meatballs before stewing in a tomato mixture. Lots of sauce which is great when serving with rice.

MEATBALLS

Ground beef	1 lb.	450 g
Dry bread crumbs	½ cup	125 mL
Egg	1	1
Soy sauce	2 tbsp.	30 mL
Onion flakes	1 tbsp.	15 mL
Salt	1 tsp.	5 mL
Pepper	¼ tsp.	1 mL
Garlic powder	¼ tsp.	1 mL

SAUCE

Canned tomatoes	28 oz.	796 mL
Chopped onion	½ cup	125 mL
Worcestershire sauce	2 tsp.	10 mL
Granulated sugar	1 tsp.	5 mL
Salt	½ tsp.	2 mL
Pepper	⅛ tsp.	0.5 mL

Meatballs: Combine all ingredients in bowl. Mix well. Shape into 24 meatballs. Set aside.

Sauce: Mix all ingredients together in saucepan. Bring to a boil. Add meatballs. Cover. Simmer gently for 30 minutes. Serves 4.

Variation: Add 1½ cups (375 mL) cooked kernel corn to Sauce and heat through. Colorful.

TOURNADOS

Filet Mignon wrapped in bacon. A pricey treat.

Fillet steaks, about 1¼ to 1½ inches (3 to 4 cm) thick	6	6
Bacon slices	6	6
Margarine (butter browns too fast)	2 tbsp.	30 mL
Pepper, sprinkle		
Mushroom caps	6	6
Bread slices	6	6

Around each steak circle a slice of bacon. Secure with wooden pick. Fry in margarine, browning both sides for about 3 minutes for rare and about 5 minutes each side for medium. Turn without piercing meat. Add more butter if needed. Sprinkle with pepper. Remove and keep hot.

Sauté mushroom caps in frying pan. Cut bread in circles slightly larger than steaks. Fry to brown both sides. Place fillets on fried bread rounds. Top each fillet with a mushroom cap. Serves 6.

SHORT RIBS

So tender and scrumptious.

Beef short ribs	3½ lbs.	1.6 kg
Tomato sauce	7½ oz.	213 mL
Ketchup	¼ cup	60 mL
Brown sugar, packed	⅓ cup	75 mL
Soy sauce	2 tbsp.	30 mL
Frozen concentrated orange juice	2 tbsp.	30 mL
Vinegar	2 tbsp.	30 mL
Worcestershire sauce	2 tbsp.	30 mL
Salt	1½ tsp.	7 mL
Pepper	½ tsp.	2 mL
Garlic powder	¼ tsp.	1 mL

Put ribs on broiler pan. Brown under broiler, for about 10 minutes. Remove from oven. Put ribs into roaster.

Mix all remaining ingredients together in bowl. Pour over ribs. Cover. Bake in 325°F (160°C) oven for 2½ to 3½ hours or longer until very tender. Bones should be loose in the meat. Reddish-brown sauce can be poured into a tall narrow container for easy fat removal before serving. Serves 4.

Spectacular!

Tenderloin of beef, cut in ½ inch (12 mm) thick slices	3 lbs.	1.35 kg
Margarine (butter browns too fast)	2 tbsp.	30 mL
Salt, sprinkle		
Pepper, sprinkle		
Sliced mushrooms	4 cups	1 L
Margarine (butter browns too fast)	¼ cup	60 mL
Water	½ cup	125 mL
Brandy, warmed (optional)	3 tbsp.	50 mL

Pound meat to about ¼ inch (6 mm) thickness.

Melt first amount of margarine in frying pan. Add meat and brown on both sides to desired degree of doneness. Sprinkle with salt and pepper.

In another pan sauté mushrooms in remaining margarine until soft. Remove from heat.

Stir in water.

Pour warm brandy over meat. Ignite. When flame dies down, remove meat to platter. Spoon mushrooms and liquid over top. Serves 6.

Variation: Rather than flaming the meat, heat canned peach halves. When hot place on platter or individual plates, cut side up, beside meat. Fill little hollows with warmed peach or apricot flavored liqueur. Ignite and carry to the table. Very pretty and impressive.

Pictured on page 17.

He made many tries at throwing a silver dollar across that river like he used to. A dollar doesn't go nearly as far as it used to.

HOMESTYLE STEW

Stew meat put to use in good family style. Top-of-the-stove method. Rich color.

Stew meat, cut up	2 lbs.	1 kg
Cooking oil	3 tbsp.	50 mL
Water	4 cups	1 L
Medium onions, cut up	2	2
Worcestershire sauce	1 tbsp.	15 mL
Ketchup	½ cup	125 mL
Salt	1 tsp.	5 mL
Basil	1 tsp.	5 mL
Sliced carrots	2 cups	500 mL
Potatoes, cut bite size	3 cups	750 mL
Frozen peas	1 cup	250 mL

Brown meat in cooking oil in large saucepan.

Add water, onion, Worcestershire sauce, ketchup, salt and basil. Cover and simmer until almost tender, about 1½ hours.

Add carrots and potatoes. Boil until tender, about 15 minutes.

Add peas. Boil about 3 minutes more. Add more water if needed. If desired, gravy may be thickened. Mix 1 tbsp. (15 mL) flour with 2 tbsp. (30 mL) water for each cup of juice. Mix smooth. Stir into boiling juice to thicken. Serves 8.

Pictured on page 89.

EASY STEWED MEAT

Quick and simple. Uses economical meat. No pre-browning.

Stew meat, cut up	2 lbs.	1 kg
Condensed cream of chicken soup	2 × 10 oz.	2 × 284 mL
Sherry (or use apple juice plus	½ cup	125 mL
2 tsp., 10 mL, red wine vinegar)		
Sliced mushrooms, drained	10 oz.	284 mL
Water	1 cup	250 mL

Put meat into small roaster. Spoon soup over top followed by sherry, mushrooms and water. Cover. Bake in 300°F (150°C) oven for 4 hours. Add more water as needed. Serves 6 to 8.

SWISS STEAK

With lots of rich reddish-brown gravy, this is meant for lots of mashed potatoes.

Round steak	2 lbs.	900 g
All-purpose flour, for coating		
Cooking oil	3 tbsp.	50 mL
Envelope dry onion soup	1	1
Condensed cream of tomato soup	2 × 10 oz.	2 × 284 mL
Sliced mushrooms with juice	10 oz.	284 mL
Water	2½ cups	600 mL

Cut meat into serving size pieces. Coat with flour and brown in cooking oil in frying pan. Put into small roaster.

Put onion soup, tomato soup, mushrooms and water into frying pan. Stir and bring to a boil. Pour over meat. Cover. Bake in 350°F (180°C) oven for 1½ to 2 hours until tender. Serves 4 to 5.

Variation: Add 1 or 2 onions, chunked or sliced, to roaster before baking.

STEAK BAKE

Delicious flavor comes from the cheese.

Blade or chuck steak, cut in serving size pieces	1¼ lbs.	560 g
Sliced onion	2 cups	500 mL
Butter or margarine	2 tbsp.	30 mL
All-purpose flour	2 tbsp.	30 mL
Salt	1 tsp.	5 mL
Pepper	¼ tsp.	1 mL
Milk	1½ cups	350 mL
Grated medium Cheddar cheese	2 cups	500 mL

Put meat into 2 quart (2.25 L) casserole. Spread onion over top.

Melt butter in saucepan over medium heat. Mix in flour, salt and pepper. Stir in milk and cheese until it boils and thickens. Pour over meat and onion. Cover. Bake in 325°F (160°C) oven until tender, about 1½ to 2 hours. Serves 4.

SWEET AND SOUR BEEF STRIPS

Another good dish that uses the less expensive steak.

Round steak, cut in thin strips	2 lbs.	900 g
Cooking oil	3 tbsp.	50 mL
Salt, sprinkle		
Water	1½ cups	375 mL
Brown sugar, packed	⅓ cup	75 mL
Cornstarch	2 tbsp.	30 mL
Pineapple chunks with juice	14 oz.	398 mL
Vinegar	¼ cup	60 mL
Soy sauce	1 tbsp.	15 mL

Brown meat strips in cooking oil. Sprinkle with salt.

Add water. Cover. Simmer until tender, about 1 hour. Check to see that it doesn't get dry, adding more water if necessary. There should not be much water left when finished.

Stir sugar and cornstarch together well in saucepan. Add pineapple and juice, vinegar and soy sauce. Stir over medium heat until it boils and thickens. Stir into beef. Serves 4 to 6.

BEEF WELLINGTON

Traditionally liver pâté is used to spread on the meat but using devilled ham from the shelf is a time saver. Individual wellingtons ensure equal pastry for every serving. May be kept chilled and baked later in the day.

Finely chopped onion	½ cup	125 mL
Finely chopped fresh mushrooms	½ cup	125 mL
Margarine (butter browns too fast)	1 tbsp.	15 mL
Salt, sprinkle		
Pepper, sprinkle		
Fillet steaks about 6 oz. (170 g) each	4	4
Margarine	1 tbsp.	15 mL
Frozen puff pastry, thawed	1 lb.	454 g
Devilled ham (or use an equal amount of liver pâté or liverwurst sausage)	3 oz.	85 g
Beaten egg (optional)		

(continued on next page)

Sauté onion and mushroom in first amount of margarine. Sprinkle with salt and pepper. Put into small dish. Set aside.

Sear steaks on both sides in remaining margarine. Cook longer if you want meat well done. Cool for a few minutes, then chill.

Cut pastry into 8 equal pieces. Roll out 1 pastry piece a little larger than steak. Spread meat with devilled ham or pâté. Place ⅛ onion-mushroom mixture on pastry, keeping in from edge. Lay steak on top. Cover with ⅛ onion-mushroom mixture. Roll out another pastry piece a little larger than steak. Lay on top of onion-mushroom mixture. Dampen edge in between and press to seal. Cut 2 vents on top. Put decorative pastry pieces on top if you have leftover small pieces. Brush with beaten egg if desired. Repeat 3 more times. Bake on baking sheet in 400°F (200°C) oven about 20 to 25 minutes until browned. Serves 4.

WIENER SCHNITZEL

Veal cutlets are always a good choice.

Veal cutlets	1½ lbs.	675 g
All-purpose flour	¼ cup	60 mL
Salt	1 tsp.	5 mL
Pepper	¼ tsp.	1 mL
Eggs	2	2
Water	1 tbsp.	15 mL
Fine dry bread crumbs	1 cup	250 mL
Margarine (butter browns too fast)	2 tbsp.	30 mL
Cooking oil	2 tbsp.	30 mL

Place cutlet between sheets of waxed paper. Pound thin. Repeat.

Mix flour with salt and pepper in shallow dish.

Beat eggs with water to make a wash.

Dip cutlets into flour mixture, then into egg wash, then into crumb mixture to coat well. These may be chilled at this point until ready to cook.

Heat margarine and cooking oil in frying pan. Cook cutlets browning on both sides turning without puncturing. Add more margarine and cooking oil if needed. Serves 4.

OVEN STEW

Just put everything in a roaster and bake for a complete meal. No pre-browning of meat.

Stew meat, cut bite size or larger	2¼ lbs.	1 kg
Medium onions, cut up	2	2
Medium potatoes, quartered	5	5
Medium carrots, quartered	5	5
Celery stalks, sliced	2	2
Canned tomatoes	28 oz.	796 mL
Minute tapioca	3 tbsp.	50 mL
Beef bouillon powder	2 tsp.	10 mL
Lemon juice	1 tsp.	5 mL
Worcestershire sauce	½ tsp.	2 mL
Salt	1 tsp.	5 mL
Pepper	½ tsp.	2 mL
Granulated sugar	1 tsp.	5 mL

Put first 5 ingredients into medium roaster.

Mix remaining ingredients together in bowl. Pour over contents in roaster. Cover. Bake in 300°F (150°C) oven for 4 hours until tender. Serves 8 to 10.

SWEDISH MEATBALLS

Serve this oldie with gravy.

Milk	¾ cup	175 mL
Dry bread crumbs	1 cup	250 mL
Finely chopped onion	⅔ cup	150 mL
Eggs, lightly beaten	2	2
Salt	1½ tsp.	7 mL
Pepper	¼ tsp.	1 mL
Garlic powder	¼ tsp.	1 mL
Allspice	¼ tsp.	1 mL
Lean ground beef	2 lbs.	900 g

Cooking oil (if frying)

Mix all ingredients together in order given. Shape into small meatballs, at least 40. Arrange on baking sheet with sides. Bake in 375°F (190°C) oven for about 15 minutes.

(continued on next page)

GRAVY

Fat in pan plus butter or margarine, if needed	¼ cup	60 mL
All-purpose flour	¼ cup	60 mL
Salt	½ tsp.	2 mL
Pepper	⅛ tsp.	0.5 mL
Milk (or half milk and half water)	2 cups	500 mL

Put fat into saucepan. Mix in flour, salt and pepper. Stir in milk over medium heat until it boils and thickens. Loosen all bits on bottom of pan. If too light in color add a bit of gravy browner. Pour over meatballs in serving bowl. Serves 6.

▬ POT ROAST ▬

Serve potatoes on the side with this old standby. For fat-free gravy trim off excess fat before cooking.

Chuck, blade or rump roast	4 lbs.	1.8 kg
Cooking oil	1 tbsp.	15 mL
Beef bouillon cube	1 × ⅕ oz.	1 × 6 g
Boiling water	2 cups	500 mL
Bay leaf (optional)	1	1
Onions, sliced	2	2
Carrots, sliced	8	8
Celery ribs, sliced	3	3
Salt	1 tsp.	5 mL
Pepper	¼ tsp.	1 mL

Brown meat well on all sides in cooking oil in large heavy saucepan or Dutch oven over medium heat.

Dissolve beef cube in boiling water. Add to saucepan along with bay leaf. Bring to a boil. Cover. Simmer gently until tender, about 3 hours. Turn 2 or 3 times.

Add onion, carrot, celery, salt and pepper. Continue to simmer for another 20 to 30 minutes until vegetables are tender. Add more water if needed. Discard bay leaf. Slice meat, serve vegetables with juice or if you want gravy, strain vegetables. Serves 8.

GRAVY: For each cup of juice strained from vegetables mix 2 tbsp. (30 mL) all-purpose flour with ¼ cup (60 mL) water until no lumps remain. Stir into boiling juice until thickened. Add salt and pepper to taste.

BASIC MEATBALLS

Use this as one of the best convenience recipes going. Freeze lots. Use as required for these and other sauce recipes in this book.

Eggs	2	2
Dry bread crumbs	1 cup	250 mL
Finely chopped onion (or use ¼ amount dried)	½ cup	125 mL
Salt	2 tsp.	10 mL
Pepper	½ tsp.	2 mL
Ground beef	2 lbs.	1 kg

Beat eggs with spoon in bowl. Add next 5 ingredients. Mix. Shape into 40 small balls. These may be browned in frying pan in fat, or bake on large baking sheet with sides in 375°F (190°C) oven for 15 to 25 minutes. Serves 6.

DILLED SAUCE

Condensed cream of mushroom soup	10 oz.	284 mL
Sour cream	¾ cup	175 mL
Beef bouillon powder	2 tsp.	10 mL
Dill weed	1 tsp.	5 mL

Mix all ingredients together in saucepan. Heat. Spoon over hot meatballs. Toss lightly to coat. Creamy dill flavor. Good.

SWEET AND SOUR SAUCE

Brown sugar, packed	2½ cups	600 mL
Water	1¼ cups	300 mL
Vinegar	⅔ cup	150 mL
Soy sauce	3 tbsp.	50 mL
Cornstarch	2½ tbsp.	40 mL
Water	3 tbsp.	50 mL

Mix sugar, first amount of water, vinegar and soy sauce together in medium saucepan. Heat over medium heat stirring occasionally until it boils.

Mix cornstarch with remaining water. Stir into sauce until it boils and thickens. Add meatballs. Simmer to heat through. Serves 6. So yummy.

(continued on next page)

SAUERBRATEN SAUCE

Beef bouillon cubes	4 × 1/5 oz.	4 × 6 g
Boiling water	3½ cups	800 mL
Red wine vinegar	1½ tbsp.	25 mL
Gingersnap crumbs	½ cup	125 mL

Dissolve beef cubes in boiling water in saucepan. Add vinegar. Stir in crumbs. Simmer until thickened. Add meatballs and continue to simmer until hot. Add more or less meatballs according to amount of sauce you want.

DEVILLED BEEF STRIPS

Turns round steak into something else! Good choice.

Round steak, cut in thin strips, 2 inches (5 cm) long	2 lbs.	900 g
All-purpose flour	⅓ cup	75 mL
Salt	1 tsp.	5 mL
Pepper	¼ tsp.	1 mL
Cooking oil	¼ cup	60 mL
Chopped onion	½ cup	125 mL
Garlic clove, minced	1	1
Margarine (butter browns too fast)	1 tbsp.	15 mL
Tomato sauce	7½ oz.	213 mL
Chopped green pepper	½ cup	125 mL
Vinegar	3 tbsp.	50 mL
Granulated sugar	1 tbsp.	15 mL
Salt	1 tsp.	5 mL
Prepared mustard	1 tsp.	5 mL
Horseradish	1 tsp.	5 mL

Put meat strips, a few at a time, into a paper or plastic bag containing flour, salt and pepper. Shake to coat. Continue until all meat strips are coated. Brown in cooking oil. Add more oil as needed. Put browned strips into 2 quart (2 L) casserole.

Put onion and garlic into pan. Add margarine and sauté until browned. Add to meat.

Mix remaining ingredients together. Pour over meat. Cover. Bake in 325°F (160°C) oven until tender, about 1½ hours. Serves 4 to 6.

MEATBALLS IN SAUCE

A mild creamy sauce from a convenient shelf product.

Egg	1	1
Milk	½ cup	125 mL
Dry bread crumbs	½ cup	125 mL
Chopped onion	¼ cup	60 mL
Salt	¾ tsp.	4 mL
Pepper	¼ tsp.	1 mL
Ground beef	1 lb.	500 g
Cooking oil	2 tbsp.	30 mL
Condensed cream of mushroom soup	10 oz.	284 mL
Milk	¼ cup	60 mL

Beat egg in bowl with spoon. Mix in next 6 ingredients in order given. Shape into 25 balls.

Brown meatballs in cooking oil in frying pan. Pile into 2 quart (2 L) casserole.

Mix soup and remaining milk together. Pour over meatballs. Bake covered in 350°F (180°C) oven for about 1 hour.

PORCUPINES: Add ¼ cup (60 mL) long grain rice to meat mixture. Shape into at least 25 balls. Place in single layer in pan allowing room for expansion. Combine soup with 1¼ cups (300 mL) water. Pour over top. Cover. Bake in 350°F (180°C) oven for 1 hour or until rice is cooked. Serves 4 to 5.

CHICKEN FRIED STEAK

Pretend you are in Texas eating one of their most popular foods.

Round steak, tenderized	2 lbs.	900 g
All-purpose flour	⅔ cup	150 mL
Salt	1 tsp.	5 mL
Pepper	¼ tsp.	1 mL
Eggs	2	2
Milk	2 tbsp.	30 mL
Cooking oil		

(continued on next page)

Cut meat into serving size pieces. Mix flour, salt and pepper together. Dip meat. Pound some flour mixture into meat.

Beat eggs and milk together.

Heat cooking oil, about ¼ inch (6 mm) deep, in frying pan. Dip meat into egg mixture then again into flour mixture. Fry slowly in cooking oil, turning, without puncturing coating, for about 30 to 40 minutes until tender and browned. Serves 4.

BEEF PARMIGIANA

Tomatoey and cheezy good.

Thinly cut round steak	1½ lbs.	675 g
Fine dry bread crumbs	⅓ cup	75 mL
Grated Parmesan cheese	⅓ cup	75 mL
Egg, fork beaten	1	1
Cooking oil	⅓ cup	75 mL
Chopped onion	1 cup	250 mL
Tomato paste	5½ oz.	156 mL
Water	2 cups	450 mL
Salt	1 tsp.	5 mL
Pepper	¼ tsp.	1 mL
Oregano	½ tsp.	2 mL
Granulated sugar	1 tsp.	5 mL
Mozzarella cheese slices	½ lb.	225 g

Cut steak into serving size pieces. Place each piece between waxed paper on bread board. Pound with meat mallet to ¼ inch (6 mm) thickness.

Mix crumbs and cheese together.

Dip meat into egg then into crumb mixture. Fry in cooking oil to brown both sides. Transfer to greased 9 × 13 inch (22 × 33 cm) baking pan.

Sauté onion in pan until soft. Add more cooking oil if necessary.

Add tomato paste, water, salt, pepper, oregano and sugar. Stir. Pour over meat.

Layer cheese over top. Cover. Bake in 350°F (180°C) oven until tender, about 1¼ to 1½ hours. Serves 4.

SPANISH MEATLOAF

Not only does this contain tomatoes, it has a deep red topping over the juicy meat. Family size loaf.

Egg	1	1
Canned tomatoes, broken up	14 oz.	398 mL
Rolled oats	1 cup	250 mL
Chopped onion	¼ cup	60 mL
Worcestershire sauce	1 tbsp.	15 mL
Salt	2 tsp.	10 mL
Pepper	¼ tsp.	1 mL
Ground beef	2 lbs.	900 g
Ketchup	½ cup	125 mL
Brown sugar, packed	⅓ cup	75 mL
Prepared mustard	1 tbsp.	15 mL

In large bowl beat egg with spoon. Mix in next 7 ingredients. Pack into 9 × 5 × 3 inch (23 × 12 × 7 cm) loaf pan.

Mix ketchup with sugar and mustard. Spread over loaf. Bake uncovered in 350°F (180°C) oven for 1¼ to 1½ hours. Serves 6 to 8.

Pictured on page107.

1. Seafood Pizza page 13
2. Sauced Patties page 76
3. Steak And Smokies page 83
4. Chicken Nuggets page 123
5. Salmon Croquettes page 26
6. Barbecue Sauced Wings page 122
7. Tuna Porcupines page 31

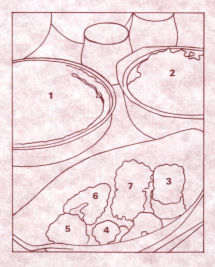

CREAMED STEAK

The end result produces exceptional gravy with an elusive flavor.

Round steak	2 lbs.	1 kg
All-purpose flour	⅓ cup	75 mL
Salt	1½ tsp.	7 mL
Pepper	¼ tsp.	1 mL
Paprika	1 tsp.	5 mL
Cooking oil	¼ cup	60 mL
Sliced onion	2 cups	500 mL
Water	2 cups	500 mL
Sour cream	½ cup	125 mL
Grated medium Cheddar cheese	¼ cup	60 mL

Pound steak with meat mallet to flatten a bit and to help tenderize. Cut into serving size pieces.

Mix flour, salt, pepper and paprika together in bowl. Set aside.

Heat cooking oil in frying pan. Add onion and sauté until browned. Remove onion to large saucepan. Dip meat into flour mixture and brown in frying pan. Add to onion.

Add water. Cover. Simmer until tender when pierced with fork, about 1 hour or so.

Add sour cream and cheese. Stir to mix. Heat through. Serves 4 to 5.

OVEN BARBECUED STEAKS

Easy to do. Ends up with a good barbecue sauce flavor.

Steak (round, blade or chuck), cut in serving size pieces	2 lbs.	1 kg
Salt, sprinkle		
Pepper, sprinkle		
Brown sugar, packed	1 cup	250 mL
Ketchup	1 cup	250 mL
Worcestershire sauce	2 tsp.	10 mL

Arrange steak pieces in small roaster or casserole in 2 or more layers. Sprinkle with salt and pepper. Cover. Bake in 300°F (150°C) oven for 3 hours. If roaster is too large, water will need to be added after 1 hour or so.

Mix sugar, ketchup and Worcestershire sauce together. Spoon over and between meat. Continue to bake covered for 30 minutes.

STEW MEAT

Try this variation for cooking stew meat or any less expensive cut of beef.

Beef stew meat (or chuck roast), cut up	2 lbs.	1 kg
Chopped onion	1½ cups	375 mL
Cooking oil	2 tbsp.	30 mL
Water	4 cups	1 L
Ketchup	½ cup	125 mL
Vinegar	2 tbsp.	30 mL
Salt	1 tsp.	5 mL
Pepper	¼ tsp.	1 mL
Worcestershire sauce	1 tbsp.	15 mL

Brown meat and onion in cooking oil in frying pan. Add more oil as needed.

Combine and add remaining ingredients. Cover. Simmer slowly for about 2 hours. Check occasionally to see if more water needs to be added. Serves 6 to 8.

MINUTE STEAK

A time saving fast-fry.

Round steak, put through tenderizer or sirloin strips, boneless and thinly sliced	1½ lbs.	675 g
Cooking oil	2 tbsp.	30 mL
Butter or margarine	4 tbsp.	60 mL
Parsley flakes	¼ tsp.	1 mL
Onion salt	¼ tsp.	1 mL

Cut steaks into 4 portions of 6 oz. (168 g) each. Spread cooking oil in very hot frying pan. Place meat in pan. Brown on one side then turn and brown other side. Be sure steaks are well chilled before browning if you don't want them cooked too much.

Mix remaining ingredients together. Shape into 4 balls. Chill.

Transfer steaks directly onto warm plates or platter. Top with butter ball. Serves 4.

ROULADEN

A recipe from Europe. Beef rolled with onion, pickles, bacon, and then tied and baked. Serve in slices. Use a thinly sliced whole round steak.

Round steak	2 lbs.	900 g
Prepared mustard	2 tbsp.	30 mL
Bacon slices	6-8	6-8
Chopped onion	1 cup	250 mL
Green pepper, finely chopped	1	1
Chopped dill pickles	1/3 cup	75 mL
Margarine (butter browns too fast)	3 tbsp.	50 mL
Water	3 cups	750 mL
Medium onion, sliced	1	1
Green pepper, slivered	1	1

Pound steak to 1/4 inch (6 mm) thickness. Spread mustard over top. Lay bacon slices over mustard followed by first amount of onion, green pepper and dill pickle. Roll like a jelly roll. Tie in several places with string.

Melt margarine in frying pan. Add beef roll and brown all sides.

Add water, remaining onion and green pepper. Simmer covered until tender, about 1 hour. Slice to serve. Remove string. Serves 6.

Variation: Individual rouladens can be made using 6 to 8 thin sandwich steaks. Use 1/2 bacon slice for each.

BAKED STEAK AND GRAVY

Put this into the oven and take out tender meat in a really good gravy.

Round or chuck steak, trimmed of excess fat	2 lbs.	900 g
Condensed cream of mushroom soup	10 oz.	284 mL
Sour cream	1 cup	250 mL
Envelope dry onion soup	1	1

Place meat, whole or in pieces, in small roaster or casserole in 2 or more layers.

Mix mushroom soup, sour cream and dry soup in small bowl. Spoon over and under meat. If roaster is too large you may need to add some water after 1 hour or so. Cover tightly. Bake in 325°F (160°C) oven for about 3 hours until tender when pierced with fork. Serves 3 to 4.

Variation: If you happen to be out of sour cream, or prefer not to use it, it will still make a good gravy.

SAUCED PATTIES

All-meat patties cooked in this sensational gravy.

Lean ground beef	2 lbs.	1 kg
Margarine (butter browns too fast)	1 tbsp.	15 mL
Salt, sprinkle		
Pepper, sprinkle		
Sour cream	1 cup	250 mL
Condensed tomato soup	10 oz.	284 mL
Envelope dry onion soup	1	1
Water	⅔ cup	175 mL
Pepper	¼ tsp.	1 mL

Form meat into about 12 patties. Fry in melted margarine in frying pan. Sprinkle with salt and pepper. Turn into 2½ quart (2.5 L) casserole.

Mix sour cream, tomato soup, onion soup, water and pepper together. Spread over meat. Cover. Bake in 350°F (180°C) oven for about 1 hour. Serves 4 to 5.

Note: Use any meatball recipe in this book for additions to the meat before shaping into patties. It will stretch the meat as well as make a softer patty.

Pictured on page 71.

ORIENTAL SHORT RIBS

With pineapple juice and soy sauce as the main cooking sauce, no wonder this is different. Good choice!

Beef short ribs	3 lbs.	1.35 kg
Pineapple juice	2 cups	500 mL
Soy sauce	⅓ cup	75 mL
Brown sugar	2 tbsp.	30 mL
Ginger	1 tsp.	5 mL
Salt	1 tsp.	5 mL
Pepper	¼ tsp.	1 mL

Put short ribs on broiler pan. Broil for about 10 minutes until browned, turning now and then. Put ribs into roaster.

Mix remaining ingredients together. Pour over meat. Cover. Bake in 325°F (160°C) oven for 2½ to 3 hours until very tender. Serves 4.

Whether company comes for dinner or for an evening, this is a festive dish to serve. Really rich looking served over a bed of buttered noodles.

All-purpose flour	⅓ cup	75 mL
Salt	½ tsp.	2 mL
Pepper	⅛ tsp.	0.5 mL
Margarine (butter browns too fast)	2 tbsp.	30 mL
Filet or sirloin steak, cut in ¼ inch (1 cm) strips	1 lb.	500 g
Thinly sliced mushrooms	1 cup	250 mL
Medium onion, chopped	1	1
Garlic powder (or 1 clove, minced)	¼ tsp.	1 mL
Butter or margarine	2 tbsp.	30 mL
Beef stock	1½ cups	375 mL
Tomato sauce	1 tbsp.	15 mL
Sour cream	1 cup	250 mL
Sherry (or alcohol-free sherry)	2 tbsp.	30 mL

Mix flour, salt and pepper together in small bowl.

Melt margarine in frying pan. Dredge meat in flour mixture and put into pan. Brown quickly on both sides.

Add mushrooms, onion, garlic powder and butter. Cook, stirring often until onion is clear. Stir in remaining flour mixture.

Add beef stock and tomato sauce. Stir until it boils and thickens. Stir in sour cream and sherry. Heat through. Serves 4.

SPEEDY ROUND STEAK

No fuss, no muss.

Round steak	1	1
Envelope dry onion soup	1	1

Put steak onto foil in roaster. Sprinkle with onion soup. Do up foil to seal. Cover. Bake in 300°F (150°C) oven for about 3 hours until tender when pierced with fork. Serves 3 to 4 depending on size of round.

FAVORITE MEATLOAF

Quick to make. Quicker to eat.

Eggs, lightly beaten	2	2
Ketchup	¾ cup	175 mL
Water or milk	½ cup	125 mL
Dry bread crumbs	1½ cups	350 mL
Envelope dry onion soup	1	1
Ground beef	2 lbs.	900 g
Salt	1 tsp.	5 mL
Pepper	½ tsp.	2 mL
Ketchup	¼ cup	60 mL

Mix first 8 ingredients together in bowl. Pack into 9 × 5 × 3 inch (23 × 12 × 7 cm) loaf pan.

Smooth ketchup over top. Bake uncovered in 350°F (180°C) oven for 1 to 1¼ hours. Serves 6 to 8.

CHEEZY MEATLOAF: Add 1 cup (250 mL) or more grated medium Cheddar cheese to meat or put cheese in a layer in center of loaf.

STEW IN FOIL

No problem to this stew. Just put vegetables on top of steak, put it in the oven and go shopping.

Chuck steak	2 lbs.	900 g
Envelope dry onion soup	1	1
Medium potatoes, quartered	4	4
Medium carrots, quartered	4	4
Medium onions, quartered	2	2

Put large piece of foil into roaster. Put meat on foil. If using meat with bone, be careful not to puncture foil. Sprinkle soup over meat. Add potatoes, carrots and onions. Seal foil. Cover. Bake in 300°F (150°C) oven for about 2½ to 3 hours until meat is tender when pierced with fork. Serves 4.

Paré Pointer

When bees get old enough do they get bee bee guns?

STUFFED MEATLOAF

Elegant. A show stopper. Extraordinary taste.

Egg, lightly beaten	1	1
Milk	½ cup	125 mL
Dry bread crumbs	¾ cup	175 mL
Salt	1¼ tsp.	6 mL
Pepper	¼ tsp.	1 mL
Ground beef	1½ lbs.	675 g
Envelope stuffing mix, prepared according to directions on box	6 oz.	170 g

Mix first 6 ingredients in bowl in order given. Pack some in bottom of 9 × 5 × 3 inch (23 × 12 × 7 cm) loaf pan to make ½ inch (12 mm) layer. Then press same thickness of meat to form walls up from layer about 2 inches (5 cm) high.

Pack stuffing mix into cavity. Pinch off any meat from walls that extends above stuffing. Add to remaining meat mixture. On waxed paper press out remaining meat mixture to the size of pan, covering from edge to edge of pan. Invert over loaf. Center, then slowly peel off paper. Tuck meat all around so that it joins walls of meat on sides. Bake uncovered in 350°F (180°C) oven for about 1 hour or so. Slice to serve. Serve with Mushroom Sauce (page 138). Serves 6.

Note: If desired, chicken bouillon powder may be replaced in Mushroom Sauce with beef bouillon powder. Both are good choices.

Pictured on page 107.

Paré Pointer

Most leaves turn in autumn but around here it is the night before a test.

GLAZED CORNED BEEF

Red meat glazed with brown sugar. Serve with cabbage for a Dinty Moore special.

Corned beef brisket	4 lbs.	1.8 kg
Water, to cover		
Large onion, sliced	1	1
Celery rib, sliced	1	1
Medium carrot, sliced	1	1
Whole cloves	4	4
Garlic clove, chopped	1	1
Brown sugar, packed	¾ cup	175 mL
Salt, sprinkle		
Paprika, sprinkle		

Place beef in large saucepan. Cover with water. Add onion, celery, carrot, cloves and garlic. Cover. Bring to a boil. Simmer until tender, about 4 hours.

Remove meat and place fat side up in small roaster. Pat brown sugar over top. Sprinkle with salt and paprika. Bake uncovered in 400°F (200°C) oven for about 10 to 15 minutes until browned. Serve with Mustard Sauce (page 42). Serves 8 to 10.

CORNED BEEF: Omit brown sugar oven glazing and you have regular corned beef.

VEAL ROAST

A tender, succulent meat.

Boneless leg of veal	4½ lbs.	2 kg
Salt, sprinkle		
Pepper, sprinkle		
Garlic powder, sprinkle		

Pat meat dry with paper towels. Sprinkle with salt, pepper and garlic powder. Rub into meat. Meat may be left without seasoning if you wish. Place in roaster. Cover or leave uncovered if you would rather. Roast in 325°F (160°C) oven for about 2½ to 3 hours. Thermometer should read 170°F (80°C). Serve with Stuffing Balls (page 38). Make gravy the same as for Standing Rib Roast (page 49), making ⅔ recipe. Serves 8 to 10.

Pictured on page 143.

PATTY BAKE

If you are lucky enough to have frozen all-meat patties in your freezer, take out some for this dish or start from scratch. A reddish brown gravy with a rich rich look to it.

Lean ground beef	2 lbs.	1 kg
Cooking oil	1 tbsp.	15 mL
Salt, sprinkle		
Pepper, sprinkle		
Condensed tomato soup	2 × 10 oz.	2 × 284 mL
Water	1¼ cups	275 mL
Envelopes dry onion soup	2	2
Pepper	¼ tsp.	1 mL

Shape ground beef into 12 patties. Fry in hot cooking oil in frying pan. After turning, sprinkle with salt and pepper. Transfer to 3 quart (3 L) casserole.

Mix tomato soup, water, onion soup and pepper together. Spoon over patties. Cover. Bake in 350°F (180°C) oven for about 1 hour. Serves 4 to 5.

Note: Add ½ cup (125 mL) each of dry bread crumbs and milk for a softer patty and to stretch meat.

GROUND BEEF ROAST

Frozen or not there's no easier way to prepare meat and gravy.

Lean ground beef	1½ lbs.	675 g
Envelope dry onion soup	1	1
Condensed cream of mushroom soup	10 oz.	284 mL

On foil in casserole or small roaster place ground beef.

Mix dry soup with mushroom soup. Spoon over meat. Do up foil. Cover. Bake in 350°F (180°C) oven for 1 to 1¼ hours. If meat is frozen there is no need to thaw. Allow 1¾ to 2 hours for cooking. Quantity of meat may be doubled. Flavor will still be good but there won't be as much gravy. To ensure enough, it is best to double both soups as well. Allow about 2 to 2¼ hours to cook 3 lbs. (1.35 kg). Serves 4.

Pictured on page 125.

CORNED BEEF PATTIES

Quick and easy. Uses canned corned beef.

Canned corned beef, flaked or ground	12 oz.	340 g
Egg	1	1
Dry bread crumbs	½ cup	125 mL
Prepared mustard	1 tsp.	5 mL
Milk, if needed to moisten	1 - 2 tbsp.	15 - 30 mL
Finely chopped onion	½ cup	125 mL
Butter or margarine	1 tbsp.	15 mL
Margarine (butter browns too fast)	1 tbsp.	15 mL

Put first 5 ingredients into bowl. Mix.

Sauté onion in butter in frying pan until soft. Add to corned beef mixture. Mix. Add a bit of milk if too dry. Shape into 10 patties.

Brown in margarine in frying pan.

CORNED BEEF BALLS: Shape into 18 balls instead of patties. Put into 2 quart (2 L) casserole. Cover with a mixture of 10 oz. (284 mL) condensed nacho cheese soup (or Cheddar cheese soup) and ½ cup (125 mL) milk. Cover. Bake in 350°F (180°C) oven for 25 to 30 minutes until hot and bubbly. Serves 3 to 4.

Pictured on page143.

BROWNED CHUCK

A delicious browned flavor. So easy. No pre-browning.

Boneless chuck or blade steak (or use stew meat) cut up	2 lbs.	1 kg
Condensed cream of mushroom soup	2 × 10 oz.	2 × 284 mL
Envelope dry onion soup	1	1
Sherry (optional but good)	½ cup	125 mL
Sliced mushrooms (optional)	10 oz.	284 mL

Put all ingredients into small roaster in order given. Cover. Bake in 325°F (160°C) oven for 3 hours or until tender when pierced with fork. Add water near end of cooking if necessary. Serves 6 to 8.

CHUCK SUPREME: Add 1 cup (250 mL) sour cream and you will have an excellent flavored favorite.

STEAK AND SMOKIES

A conversation piece. Neat looking.

Round steak, thinly cut	2 lbs.	900 g
Smokies (smoked sausages)	6	6
Cooking oil	3 tbsp.	50 mL
Medium onion, chopped	1	1
Salt, sprinkle		
Pepper, sprinkle		
Beef bouillon powder	4 tsp.	20 mL
Hot water	2 cups	450 mL

Pound meat to ¼ inch (6 mm) thickness or less. Cut into 6 pieces. Place a smokey on each piece of meat and roll up. Secure with wooden picks or string.

Brown rolls in hot oil along with onion in frying pan. Sprinkle with salt and pepper.

Dissolve bouillon powder in hot water. Pour over meat. Cover. Simmer until tender, about 35 to 45 minutes. Slice into 1 inch (2.5 cm) pieces. Serves 6.

Pictured on page 71.

STEAK FRY

An all-time favorite.

Steak (T-bone, porterhouse, club or sirloin) 1 inch (2.5 cm) thick, allowing ½ to ¾ lb. (225 to 340 g) per serving	6	6

Cut off excess fat from meat. Fry fat in hot pan until well greased. Remove fat. Add steak. Sear on both sides turning often. Continue to fry at a bit lower heat than used for searing. It will take about 8 minutes for rare and up to 20 minutes for well done.

VEAL STEAK: Cook as above.

LAMB CHOPS: Cook as above.

PORK CHOPS: Cook as above but cook until no pink remains.

VEAL OSCAR

An elegant meal for entertaining.

Veal steaks, boneless	4	4
All-purpose flour, for coating		
Margarine (butter browns too fast)	3 tbsp.	50 mL
Fresh asparagus spears	12	12
Boiling salted water		
Crabmeat	½ lb.	225 g
BEARNAISE SAUCE		
White wine	2 tbsp.	30 mL
(or alcohol-free white wine)		
Tarragon vinegar	1 tbsp.	15 mL
Chopped green onion	1 tbsp.	15 mL
Dried tarragon leaves	1 tsp.	5 mL
Pepper	¼ tsp.	1 mL
Egg yolks	3	3
Butter (not margarine)	½ cup	125 mL

Pound meat between sheets of waxed paper until thin. Dip into flour. Brown both sides in margarine in frying pan until cooked. Keep hot.

Cook asparagus in salted water until tender, about 10 to 15 minutes. Drain. Heat crabmeat.

BEARNAISE SAUCE: Bring wine, vinegar, green onion, tarragon leaves and pepper to a boil in small saucepan. Remove from heat. Cover.

Put egg yolks into blender. Blend together. With blender running add butter very slowly in a thin stream. Add tarragon mixture. Blend 6 seconds. Keep hot over hot water. If sauce curdles, whisk in 1 to 2 tbsp. (15 to 30 mL) water.

To serve, place 3 asparagus spears on each steak along with crab. Spoon Bearnaise Sauce over top. Makes 1 cup (225 mL). Serves 4.

Paré Pointer

When the hungry monkey showed up, the banana split.

Two racks of lamb are used to form this roast with stuffing in between. Showy. Serve with mint jelly or sauce.

Racks of lamb, each with 6 or 7 ribs	**2**	**2**
Envelope stuffing mix, prepared according to directions on box	**6 oz.**	**170 g**

Ask butcher to chine or crack the backbone to make serving easier. With fat forming outside walls, interlace bones like you fold your fingers together. A tunnel will form to hold dressing. Using string, tie together at 2 to 3 cutlet intervals.

Spoon stuffing into hollow. This will use about ½ envelope. Rest may be served on the side. Place meat in roaster with bone ends up. Cover ends of bone with foil if desired to prevent burning. Cover. Roast in 350°F (180°C) oven until cooked, about 1½ hours. Transfer to plate. Remove string and foil. Slice one rib wide, cutting straight down so as to form guard on plate with stuffing in center. Serves 4 if racks are a good size.

GRAVY

Lamb fat	**⅓ cup**	**75 mL**
All-purpose flour	**⅓ cup**	**75 mL**
Salt	**1 tsp.**	**5 mL**
Pepper	**¼ tsp.**	**1 mL**
Drippings plus water	**2½ cups**	**600 mL**

Pour all liquid from roaster into narrow container. Return measured amount of fat to pan. Mix in flour, salt and pepper. Add drippings and water. Stir over medium heat until it boils and thickens. If gravy is pale add a bit of gravy browner. Taste for salt and pepper adding as needed. Makes 2½ cups (350 mL).

Pictured on cover.

RACK OF LAMB: Lay 5 to 7 rib racks curved side down in roaster. Sprinkle lightly with garlic powder and thyme or leave plain. Roast as above.

Paré Pointer

Eat lamb. Ten thousand coyotes can't be wrong.

STUFFED LEG OF LAMB

Lamb at its best with stuffing as well. Lamb shoulder may be cooked in the same way. Serve with mint sauce or jelly.

Leg of lamb, boned	5½ lbs.	2.5 kg
Salt, sprinkle		
Pepper, sprinkle		
STUFFING		
Butter or margarine	3 tbsp.	50 mL
Chopped onion	½ cup	125 mL
Chopped celery	½ cup	125 mL
Butter or margarine, cut up	½ cup	125 mL
Salt	½ tsp.	2 mL
Pepper	⅛ tsp.	0.5 mL
Poultry seasoning	1 tsp.	5 mL
Parsley flakes	1 tsp.	5 mL
Dry bread crumbs	3 cups	700 mL

Sprinkle inside of meat with salt and pepper.

Stuffing: Melt first amount of butter in large frying pan. Add onion and celery. Sauté until onion is clear and soft. Remove from heat.

Add remaining butter, salt, pepper, poultry seasoning, and parsley. Stir. Add crumbs. Mix together. Place stuffing on meat. Pull meat together in a roll. Tie with string. Place in roaster. Bake covered (or uncovered if you wish) in 325°F (170°C) oven for 35 minutes per pound for well done lamb. Thermometer should read 180°F (82°C). This will take about 3½ hours. If cooking uncovered you will need to baste now and then. Prepared orange juice gives a nice touch. Serves 8 or more if leg is large.

GRAVY		
Fat from roaster	¼ cup	60 mL
All-purpose flour	¼ cup	60 mL
Salt	1 tsp.	5 mL
Pepper	¼ tsp.	1 mL
Water	2 cups	500 mL

(continued on next page)

Remove roast to platter. Pour all drippings into narrow container. Spoon off fat. Put required amount into roaster. Mix in flour, salt and pepper. Put remaining juice (no fat) into measuring cup plus water to make given amount needed. Add to flour mixture. Heat and stir until boiling. Scrape brown bits from bottom of pan. If needed, add a few drops of gravy browner. Check seasoning. Add more water if too thick. Makes 2 cups (500 mL). Double for serving 8.

BUTTERFLIED LAMB: After bone is removed from leg, lay meat flat in roaster. Roast.

STUFFED LAMB SHOULDER: Prepare and roast like the leg. Less cooking time may be needed due to the shoulder being smaller than the leg.

IRISH STEW

You will want to serve colorful vegetables with this light colored stew. See variation to cook as regular stew.

Lamb neck meat, cubed	2 lbs.	1 kg
Large onions	2	2
Potatoes, peeled and sliced	2 lbs.	1 kg
or shredded		
Salt, sprinkle		
Pepper, sprinkle		
Parsley flakes, sprinkle		
Water		

Use large saucepan or Dutch oven to boil on top of stove. Use large casserole to bake in oven. Layer meat, onion, potato, then another layer of each. Sprinkle each layer with salt and pepper. Sprinkle with parsley.

Fill saucepan, half way up food, with water. Bring to a boil. Cover and simmer slowly until meat is tender, about 2 to 2½ hours or cover and bake in 350°F (180°C) oven for about 3 to 3½ hours until meat is tender. Serves 8.

Variation: Brown meat first then assemble, adding carrots and turnip for both color and flavor.

HAM TOMATO LOAF

This moist ham and hamburger loaf is sparked with a delicious tangy sauce. Slices well for sandwiches when cold.

Ground ham	1 lb.	450 g
Ground beef	1 lb.	450 g
Condensed tomato soup	½ × 10 oz.	½ × 284 mL
Milk	⅓ cup	75 mL
Egg	1	1
Dry bread crumbs	¾ cup	175 mL
Finely chopped onion	½ cup	125 mL
SAUCE		
Condensed tomato soup	½ × 10 oz.	½ × 284 mL
Brown sugar, packed	½ cup	125 mL
Vinegar	¼ cup	60 mL

Mix first 7 ingredients together in bowl. Pack into 9 × 5 × 3 inch (23 × 12 × 7 cm) loaf pan.

Sauce: Mix soup with sugar and vinegar. Spread over meat mixture. Bake uncovered in 350°F (180°C) oven for 1¼ to 1½ hours. Serves 6 to 8.

Pictured on page 143.

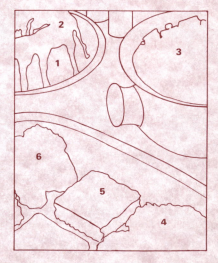

BARBECUED PORK CHOPS

Barbecued in the oven the easy way. Reddish color. Good.

Pork chops	16	16
Margarine (butter browns too fast)	2 - 4 tbsp.	30 - 60 mL
Ketchup	¾ cup	175 mL
Water	1 cup	225 mL
Vinegar	2 tbsp.	30 mL
Worcestershire sauce	1 tbsp.	15 mL
Chopped onion	1 cup	250 mL
Dry mustard powder	1 tsp.	5 mL
Chili powder	1 tsp.	5 mL
Brown sugar	2 tbsp.	30 mL
Salt	1 tsp.	5 mL
Pepper	¼ tsp.	1 mL
Paprika	1 tsp.	5 mL
Garlic powder	¼ tsp.	1 mL

Brown pork chops in margarine in frying pan.

Mix remaining ingredients together. Cover bottom of roaster with single layer of chops. Spoon some sauce over. Repeat. Cover. Bake in 350°F (180°C) oven for about 1 hour. Remove cover. Bake 15 minutes more. Serves 8 people, 2 chops each.

PORK CHOPS WITH LEMON

A very different flavor for chops. Try this instead of your usual method.

Pork chops	4	4
Cooking oil	1 tbsp.	15 mL
Salt, sprinkle		
Pepper, sprinkle		
Medium onion, sliced	1	1
Lemon, thinly sliced	1	1
Medium green pepper, slivered	1	1
Granulated sugar	1 tsp.	5 mL
Tomato juice	2 cups	450 mL

Brown chops in hot cooking oil in frying pan. Sprinkle with salt and pepper.

Add remaining ingredients. Cover. Simmer until very tender, about 1 hour. Serves 4.

HAM SQUARES

A glistening glaze covers this ham. A good use for leftover ham or use canned ham.

Cooked ham, ground	2 cups	500 mL
Dry bread crumbs	¾ cup	175 mL
Milk	½ cup	125 mL
Eggs, fork beaten	2	2
Finely chopped onion	½ cup	125 mL
Finely chopped celery	¼ cup	60 mL
Prepared mustard	2 tsp.	10 mL
Worcestershire sauce	1 tsp.	5 mL
GLAZE		
Brown sugar, packed	¾ cup	175 mL
All-purpose flour	2 tbsp.	30 mL
Salt	¼ tsp.	1 mL
Water	1 cup	225 mL
Vinegar	¼ cup	60 mL

Mix first 8 ingredients together in large bowl. Pack into greased 8 × 8 inch (20 × 20 cm) pan.

Glaze: Mix sugar, flour and salt together in small saucepan. Add water and vinegar. Heat and stir over medium heat until it boils and thickens. Pour over loaf. Bake uncovered in 350°F (180°C) oven for about 45 minutes. Cut into squares. Serves 4.

Pictured on page 89.

SAUSAGE FRY

When boiled first, much of the fat is removed from the sausages. Good gravy.

Sausages	1 lb.	454 g
Cold water		
Medium onion, sliced	1	1
Granulated sugar	1 tsp.	5 mL
All-purpose flour	2 tbsp.	30 mL
Thyme	¼ tsp.	1 mL
Water	1 cup	225 mL
Salt	½ tsp.	2 mL

(continued on next page)

Cover sausages with water in frying pan. Cover. Bring to a boil. Drain. Brown sausages being careful not to overcook and harden them. Remove to dish.

Add onion and sugar to frying pan. Fry until browned. Stir often.

Mix in flour and thyme. Stir in water and salt until it boils and thickens. Add sausage. Heat through. Serves 3 to 4.

CURRIED HAM ROLLS

Nice for a lighter meal or for a second meat.

CURRY SAUCE

Butter or margarine	¼ cup	60 mL
All-purpose flour	¼ cup	60 mL
Curry powder	2 tsp.	10 mL
Salt	1 tsp.	5 mL
Milk	2 cups	500 mL
Raisins	1 cup	250 mL

ROLLS

Cooked rice	2 cups	450 mL
Curry sauce (above)	½ cup	125 mL
Finely chopped onion	2 tbsp.	30 mL
Parsley flakes	1 tsp.	5 mL
Ham slices, ⅛ inch (0.5 cm) thick	12	12

Curry Sauce: Melt butter in saucepan. Mix in flour, curry powder, and salt. Stir in milk and raisins until it boils and thickens.

Rolls: Mix rice, curry sauce, onion and parsley together.

Divide rice mixture and spread on ham slices. If using very thin sandwich-type ham, use 2 to 3 to obtain desired thickness. Roll up and place in shallow greased baking dish, seam side down. Spoon remaining Curry Sauce over top adding a bit more milk if desired. Bake uncovered in 325°F (160°C) oven for 25 to 30 minutes until heated through. Makes 12 rolls.

Pictured on page 35.

ROAST PORK LOIN

A favorite roast. Serve with applesauce for a perfect condiment.

Loin of pork	4½ lbs.	2 kg
Salt, sprinkle		
Pepper, sprinkle		
Sage or poultry seasoning, sprinkle		
GRAVY		
All-purpose flour	⅔ cup	150 mL
Salt	1 tsp.	5 mL
Pepper	¼ tsp.	1 mL
Water	5 cups	1.12 L

Lay pork loin, fat side up, in roaster. Sprinkle with salt, pepper and sage. Rub in with your hands. Cover. Roast in 350°F (180°C) oven for about 2½ hours or until tender and no pink juice runs out when pierced with a fork.

Gravy: Remove roast from pan. Keep warm. Remove fat leaving ⅔ cup (150 mL) in roaster. Mix in flour, salt and pepper over medium heat. Stir in water until it boils and thickens. Check for salt and pepper. Add a bit of gravy browner if needed. Slice between ribs to serve 8 to 9.

BONELESS PORK LOIN: Roast as for Pork Loin. The same weight will serve about 2 more people.

BAKED PORK TENDERLOIN

Baked to perfection in a delicious sauce.

Whole pork tenderloins	4	4
Margarine (butter browns too fast)	2 tbsp.	30 mL
SAUCE		
Butter or margarine	3 tbsp.	50 mL
Chopped onion	3 tbsp.	50 mL
All-purpose flour	3 tbsp.	50 mL
Condensed beef consommé	10 oz.	284 mL
Water	1¼ cups	275 mL
Vinegar	1 - 2 tsp.	5 - 10 mL
Prepared mustard	1 - 2 tsp.	5 - 10 mL

(continued on next page)

Brown tenderloins in margarine in frying pan. Transfer to baking pan or small roaster.

Sauce: Melt butter in frying pan. Add onion. Sauté until soft. Remove from heat.

Mix in flour. Stir in consommé until smooth. Heat until it boils and thickens, loosening any bits in pan. Add water, vinegar and mustard. Pour over meat. Cover. Bake in 350°F (180°C) oven until no pink remains, about 1 to 1½ hours. Slice in medallions, ¼ inch (6 mm) slices, to serve. Pour sauce into narrow container such as a measuring cup to easily spoon off fat. Serves 8 to 10.

RAISIN PORK STEAK

A super tasty sauce comes from this apple and raisin pork.

Pork shoulder steak	3 lbs.	1.35 kg
Margarine (butter browns too fast)	2 tbsp.	30 mL
Salt	½ tsp.	2 mL
Sage	½ tsp.	2 mL
Apples, peeled, cored and sliced in ¼ inch (6 mm) slices	3	3
Brown sugar, packed	¼ cup	60 mL
All-purpose flour	¼ cup	60 mL
Salt	½ tsp.	2 mL
Water	2 cups	450 mL
Vinegar	1 tbsp.	15 mL
Raisins	½ cup	125 mL

Trim excessive fat from meat. Brown steak in margarine in frying pan. Transfer steak to small roaster. Sprinkle with salt and sage.

Arrange apples over steak. Sprinkle with sugar.

Mix flour and salt into fat in frying pan. Stir in water, vinegar and raisins and heat until it boils and thickens. Pour over meat. Bake uncovered in 350°F (180°C) oven for about 1 to 1¼ hours until tender. Serves 6.

Paré Pointer

Are all the cows that are lying down ground beef?

QUICK OVEN PORK CHOPS

No pre-browning necessary. Makes a tasty sauce. Chops have a mild lemony flavor.

Pork chops, trimmed of fat	4	4
Ketchup	¼ cup	60 mL
Water	¼ cup	60 mL
Brown sugar	¼ cup	60 mL
Lemon slices	4	4

Arrange chops in baking pan.

Mix ketchup, water and sugar together. Pour over chops.

Lay 1 lemon slice on top of each chop. Cover. Bake in 350°F (180°C) oven for about 1½ hours until tender when pierced with fork. Serves 4.

Variation: Add an onion slice to each chop. Lemon flavor is cut somewhat. A good addition.

SAUSAGE PATTIES

Served with a milk gravy, this is a good anytime dish.

Sausage meat	1 lb.	454 g
Cooking oil	1 tbsp.	15 mL
GRAVY		
All-purpose flour	2 tbsp.	30 mL
Salt	½ tsp.	2 mL
Milk	1 cup	250 mL

Shape meat into patties. Brown in frying pan in cooking oil until no pink remains. Drain on paper towels. Serves 3 to 4.

Gravy: Drain off fat leaving 2 tbsp. (30 mL) in pan. Mix in flour and salt. Stir in milk until it boils and thickens. Loosen all bits from bottom of pan. Add more milk if desired. Makes 1 cup (250mL).

FRIED SAUSAGES: Puncture skin here and there. Pan fry until no pink remains.

BAKED SAUSAGES: Puncture skin in several places. Put into baking pan. Add water so bottom of pan is just covered. Bake uncovered in 350°F (180°C) oven until crispy, about 35 minutes.

BEST CHOP BAKE

Very different in appearance with sour cream and mushrooms over top. No pre-browning needed. Great time saver.

Thick pork chops, trimmed of fat	6	6
Butter or margarine	3 tbsp.	50 mL
All-purpose flour	2 tbsp.	30 mL
Beef bouillon powder	2 tbsp.	30 mL
Dry onion flakes	2 tbsp.	30 mL
Milk	1¼ cups	250 mL
Sour cream	1 cup	250 mL
Canned sliced mushrooms, drained	10 oz.	284 mL

Arrange chops in small roaster.

Melt butter in saucepan over medium heat. Mix in flour, bouillon powder and onion flakes. Stir in milk until it boils and thickens. Pour over meat.

Spoon sour cream over top. Sprinkle with mushrooms. Cover. Bake in 325°F (180°C) oven until tender, about 1½ hours. Serves 6.

EASY PORK CHOPS

So moist and good.

Pork chops	8	8
Cooking oil	2 tbsp.	30 mL
Salt, sprinkle		
Pepper, sprinkle		
Condensed cream of mushroom soup	10 oz.	284 mL
Worcestershire sauce	2 tsp.	10 mL
Paprika	1 tsp.	5 mL

Brown chops in oil in frying pan. Sprinkle with salt and pepper. Put into small roaster.

Stir soup, Worcestershire sauce and paprika together. Spoon over chops. Cover. Bake in 350°F (180°C) oven for about 1½ hours until tender. Makes 8 servings if chops are thick or serves 4 people, 2 chops each.

HAM CRÊPES

These crêpes contain not only ham but a rich mushroom sauce as well.

FILLING

Mushrooms, sliced	1½ lbs.	675 g
Butter or margarine	2 - 4 tbsp.	30 - 60 mL
All-purpose flour	1 tbsp.	15 mL
Heavy cream	½ cup	125 mL

SAUCE

All-purpose flour	1½ tbsp.	25 mL
Butter or margarine	1½ tbsp.	25 mL
Salt	¼ tsp.	1 mL
Pepper, light sprinkle		
Rich milk	1 cup	250 mL
Thin cooked ham slices	12	12
Prepared Crêpes, see page 15		
Dill weed, sprinkle (or grated Swiss cheese, about 1 cup, 250 mL)		

Filling: Sauté mushrooms in butter for about 5 minutes.

Sprinkle flour over mushrooms. Stir. Add cream. Stir to thicken. Cool.

Sauce: Mix flour in butter over medium heat. Add salt, pepper and milk. Stir until it boils and thickens.

Lay ham slices over crêpes. Spoon ¼ cup (60 mL) mushroom mixture over end of each ham slice. Roll and place in 9 × 13 inch (22 × 33 cm) baking dish. Pour sauce over all.

Sprinkle with dill weed or cheese. Bake covered in 400°F (200°C) oven for 15 minutes until hot. Serves 6.

Pictured on page 125.

No matter what kind of children the Invisible Man and Woman have, bet they wouldn't be much to look at.

BARBECUED FLAVORED PORK CHOPS

Cook these indoors and have a good barbecued flavor.

Pork chops, trimmed of fat	6	6
Chili sauce	3 tbsp.	50 mL
Brown sugar	3 tbsp.	50 mL
Vinegar	3 tbsp.	50 mL
Water	6 tbsp.	100 mL
Dry mustard powder	2 tbsp.	30 mL

Arrange pork chops in baking pan.

Mix remaining ingredients together. Spoon over meat. Cover. Bake in 350°F (180°C) oven for 1½ hours. Bake without cover for the last 15 minutes. Serves 6.

Note: Stir hot water into sauce remaining in pan for a tasty gravy.

BARBECUED FLAVORED RIBS: Use spareribs in place of chops. Very tasty.

COATED BAKED PORK CHOPS

A very convenient oven method which gives a nice looking coated chop. Worry free. No pre-browning necessary. Good.

Crushed corn flakes	½ cup	125 mL
Grated Parmesan cheese	⅔ cup	150 mL
Salt	1½ tsp.	7 mL
Pepper	¼ tsp.	1 mL
Paprika	½ tsp.	2 mL
Egg	1	1
Milk	2 tbsp.	30 mL
Large pork chops	6	6

Mix first 5 ingredients together in medium size bowl.

Fork beat egg and milk together in small bowl.

Dip chops into egg mixture and coat with crumbs. Arrange on greased baking pan. Bake uncovered in 350°F (180°C) oven for about 1¼ hours until tender. Serves 6.

PORK STEAK WITH GRAVY

After browning, these are simmered in the frying pan until tender. A good gravy is the bonus when finished.

Pork shoulder steaks, serving size portions	6	6
Margarine (butter browns too fast)	2 tbsp.	30 mL
Salt, sprinkle		
Pepper, sprinkle		
Sliced onion	1 cup	250 mL
Water	1¼ cups	275 mL
Sour cream	1¼ cups	275 mL
Paprika	2 tsp.	10 mL
Dill seed	1 tsp.	5 mL

Brown meat in margarine in frying pan. Sprinkle with salt and pepper. Remove from pan. Brown onion adding more butter if needed. Return meat to frying pan.

Mix water, sour cream, paprika and dill seed together. Pour over meat and onion. Cover. Simmer slowly for about 1 hour until tender. Add more water if needed. Serves 6.

OVEN PORK CHOPS

Each chop has its own bit of rice with an onion slice on top. Serve with its reddish colored sauce.

Pork chops	6	6
Cooking oil	1 tbsp.	15 mL
Salt, sprinkle		
Pepper, sprinkle		
Long grain rice	6 tbsp.	100 mL
Onion slices	6	6
Condensed cream of tomato soup	10 oz.	284 mL
Water	½ cup	125 mL

Brown chops in hot oil in frying pan. Sprinkle with salt and pepper. Transfer to small roaster.

Place 1 tbsp. (15 mL) rice on top of each chop followed by 1 onion slice.

Mix soup with water. Pour over all. Cover. Bake in 350°F (180°C) oven until tender and rice is cooked, about 1½ hours. Serves 6.

HAM PATTIES

The quickest way to use leftover ham. The sauce enhances it greatly.

Ground ham	2 cups	500 mL
Mashed potato	2 cups	500 mL
Parsley flakes	1 tsp.	5 mL
Onion flakes, crushed	2 tsp.	10 mL

Mix all ingredients together. Shape into patties. Brown well on both sides in well greased frying pan. Serve with Mustard Sauce (page 42). Makes 12 medium patties. Serves 4.

JIFFY PORK CHOPS

Juicy, onion flavored, no work chops. No pre-browning.

Pork chops, thick, trimmed of fat	4	4
Envelope dry onion soup	1	1
Water	1 cup	250 mL

Arrange chops in baking dish.

Mix onion soup with water. Spoon over meat. For easy clean up, use foil in baking dish. Fold over to seal. Cover. Bake in 350°F (180°C) oven for about 1½ hours until tender when pierced with fork. Serves 4.

CHILI PORK STEAK

A change of good taste. Colorful.

Pork shoulder steaks	4	4
Margarine (butter browns too fast)	2 tbsp.	30 mL
Condensed cream of tomato soup	10 oz.	284 mL
Chili powder	2 tsp.	10 mL
Oregano	¼ tsp.	1 mL
Worcestershire sauce	1 tsp.	5 mL

Brown steaks in margarine in frying pan.

Add soup, chili powder, oregano and Worcestershire sauce. Mix a little. Cover. Simmer slowly until tender, about 45 minutes. Serves 4.

STUFFED PORK CHOPS

A difficult choice to make. Whether corn or apple is used in the stuffing, you will find both are delicious.

Pork chops, at least 1 inch (2.5 cm) thick	4	4
Salt, sprinkle		
Pepper, sprinkle		
Dry bread crumbs	1 cup	250 mL
Cooked kernel corn (or use twice as much diced apple)	¼ cup	60 mL
Onion flakes	1 tbsp.	15 mL
Poultry seasoning	½ tsp.	2 mL
Parsley flakes	½ tsp.	2 mL
Celery salt	⅛ tsp.	0.5 mL
Salt (optional)	⅛ tsp.	0.5 mL
Butter or margarine, melted	1 tbsp.	15 mL
Water	2 tbsp.	30 mL

Carefully cut a slit in one end of chop to form a pocket for stuffing, or have your butcher do it. Sprinkle with salt and pepper on both sides. Rub into meat.

Mix remaining ingredients in bowl in order given. Stuff chops. Fasten with wooden picks. Place in roaster. Cover. Bake in 350°F (180°C) oven for about 1½ hours until tender and no pink juice runs out when pierced with fork. To brown nicely before serving, brush with melted butter and place under broiler. Serve with Mushroom Sauce, below. Serves 6.

Mushroom Sauce: Mix ⅓ cup (75 mL) milk with 10 oz. (284 mL) condensed cream of mushroom soup. Heat until bubbling hot. Makes 1½ cups (350 mL).

TERIYAKI CHOPS

A popular flavor. No wonder these are so good.

Brown sugar, packed	¾ cup	175 mL
Soy sauce	¼ cup	60 mL
Chopped onion	¼ cup	60 mL
Lemon, thinly sliced	1	1
Lemon juice	1 tbsp.	15 mL
Pork chops, trimmed	6	6
Water	½ cup	125 mL

(continued on next page)

Combine first 5 ingredients together in large flat pan. Stir well.

Add chops in single layer. Let stand 1 hour. Turn often so all meat marinates.

Put chops into small roaster. Add water to marinade. Pour over chops. Cover. Bake in 325°F (160°C) oven until tender, about 1½ hours. To make sauce, stir some more hot water if necessary into pan after removing pork chops. Stir, being sure to get all bits and color from sides of pan. Serves 6.

GLAZED RIBS

These have a gorgeous glaze with a flavor to match.

Pork back ribs	3 lbs.	1.35 kg
SAUCE		
Maple syrup (see Note)	¾ cup	175 mL
Ketchup	2 tbsp.	30 mL
Brown sugar	2 tbsp.	30 mL
Cider vinegar	1 tbsp.	15 mL
Worcestershire sauce	1 tbsp.	15 mL
Salt	½ tsp.	2 mL
Dry mustard powder	½ tsp.	2 mL

Cut ribs in 2-rib widths. Place in roaster. Cover and roast in 425°F (220°C) oven for 30 minutes. Pour off grease. Turn oven down to 325°F (160°C).

Sauce: Measure all ingredients into saucepan. Heat and stir until it begins to boil. Pour over ribs. Roast, uncovered in 325°F (160°C) oven for 1 hour. Turn ribs occasionally. Serves 4.

Note: As a substitute for maple syrup, put 2 tbsp. (30 mL) water and 1 tsp. (5 mL) maple flavoring into a measuring cup. Add corn syrup to measure ¾ cup (175 mL). Maple flavored pancake syrup may also be used.

Paré Pointer

The way that young lovely thing sweeps the room with a glance is about all the housework she's interested in.

BAKED STUFFED SPARERIBS

Simply put stuffing between two layers of ribs and bake.

Spareribs (crack long ribs)	6 lbs.	2.7 kg
Butter or margarine	3 tbsp.	50 mL
Chopped onion	2 cups	450 mL
Egg	1	1
Dry bread crumbs	3 cups	700 mL
Poultry seasoning	1 tsp.	5 mL
Celery salt	½ tsp.	2 mL
Salt	1 tsp.	5 mL
Pepper	¼ tsp.	1 mL
Milk, enough to moisten if needed		

Lay ½ ribs in strip in roaster.

Melt butter in frying pan. Add onion. Sauté until clear and soft.

Beat egg in bowl. Add next 5 ingredients. Add onion. Mix. If dry, add a bit of milk to moisten. Spoon over ribs. Cover with other strip of ribs. Cover. Bake in 350°F (180°C) oven until tender, about 2½ hours. Serves 8.

BARBECUED SPARERIBS

An outdoor flavor enjoyed any time of year. Very tasty.

Spareribs	4 lbs.	1.8 kg
Large onion, sliced	1	1
Ketchup	1 cup	250 mL
Water	1 cup	250 mL
Brown sugar, packed	½ cup	125 mL
Vinegar	⅓ cup	75 mL
Worcestershire sauce	2 tbsp.	30 mL
Chili powder	½ tsp.	2 mL
Salt	½ tsp.	2 mL
Prepared mustard	1 tsp.	5 mL
Garlic powder	¼ tsp.	1 mL

Cut ribs into serving size pieces. Put into roaster. Scatter onion over top.

Mix remaining ingredients together well. Pour over all. Cover. Bake in 350°F (180°C) oven for 1½ hours. Uncover and bake for 20 to 30 minutes more. Serves 6.

ORANGE PORK

Delicate orange flavor. The addition of prunes and oranges looks colorful.

Pork shoulder steak or chops	3 lbs.	1.35 kg
Salt, sprinkle		
Pepper, sprinkle		
Prepared orange juice	2 cups	450 mL
Orange marmalade	2 tbsp.	30 mL
Pitted dried prunes	12 - 18	12 - 18
Mandarin oranges, drained,	12 oz.	341 mL
discard juice		

Trim off extra fat from meat. Fry fat in frying pan to render. Brown meat in fat in frying pan. Sprinkle with salt and pepper.

Add orange juice, marmalade and prunes. Stir a bit. Cover. Simmer until tender, about 1 hour.

Add all or only part of the oranges. Heat through. Serves 6.

Note: If serving with rice you may want to thicken juice. To each 1 cup (225 mL) juice add a mixture of 1 tbsp. (15 mL) each of cornstarch and water. Boil to thicken.

PORK CHOPS WITH GRAVY

A delicious gravy is in the making as these chops cook.

Pork chops, large size	6	6
Margarine (butter browns too fast)	2 tbsp.	30 mL
Salt, sprinkle		
Pepper, sprinkle		
Condensed cream of chicken soup	10 oz.	284 mL
Ketchup	3 tbsp.	50 mL
Finely chopped onion	1/3 cup	75 mL
Worcestershire sauce	1 tbsp.	15 mL

Brown pork chops on both sides in margarine in frying pan. Sprinkle with salt and pepper. Arrange in baking dish.

Mix remaining ingredients together. Spoon over meat. Cover. Bake in 350°F (180°C) oven for about 1½ hours until tender when pierced with fork. Serves 6.

SWEET AND SOUR RIBS

Delicious served with or without the sauce.

All-purpose flour	⅓ cup	75 mL
Cornstarch	1½ tbsp.	25 mL
Granulated sugar	2 tbsp.	30 mL
Salt	2 tsp.	10 mL
Spareribs, cut small	3 lbs.	1.35 kg
Margarine (butter browns too fast)	¼ cup	60 mL
Brown sugar, packed	2¼ cups	500 mL
Water	2¼ cups	500 mL
Vinegar	1⅛ cups	250 mL
Worcestershire sauce	1 tbsp.	15 mL

Mix first 4 ingredients together.

Coat ribs in flour mixture. Brown in margarine in frying pan.

In large saucepan mix sugar, water, vinegar and Worcestershire sauce. Add ribs. Bring to a boil. Cover. Simmer for about 30 minutes. Stir once or twice. Serves 4.

Note: To thicken sauce, pour into narrow container, spoon off fat. You will have about 1⅔ cups (375 mL) juice. Mix 2 tbsp. (30 mL) cornstarch with same amount of water. Mix and boil with juice to thicken. Serve over rice or serve the ribs in the sauce.

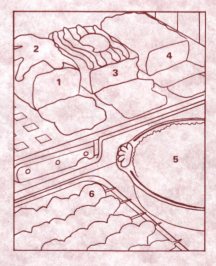

PORK SCHNITZEL

Served with Dill Sauce this is unusual and also exceptionally good.

Boneless pork loin cutlets	6	6
Egg	1	1
Milk	2 tbsp.	30 mL
Fine dry bread crumbs	½ cup	125 mL
Salt	1 tsp.	5 mL
Pepper	¼ tsp.	1 mL
Paprika	1 tsp.	5 mL
Margarine (butter browns too fast)	¼ cup	50 mL

If not already tenderized, place meat between sheets of waxed paper. Pound with meat mallet to a thickness of ¼ inch (6 mm). Snip edges to prevent curling.

Fork beat egg and milk together.

Mix crumbs, salt, pepper and paprika together.

Heat margarine in frying pan. Dip meat into egg mixture then into crumbs. Fry, browning both sides, about 5 minutes per side or until no pink remains. Spoon Dill Sauce over top or serve on the side. Serves 6.

DILL SAUCE

All-purpose flour	2 tbsp.	30 mL
Butter or margarine	2 tbsp.	30 mL
Dill weed	½ tsp.	2 mL
Chicken bouillon cubes	2 × ⅕ oz.	2 × 6 g
Boiling water	1½ cups	375 mL
Sour cream	1 cup	250 mL

Add flour, butter and dill weed to frying pan in which meat was cooked. Mix together.

Dissolve bouillon cubes in water. Add and stir until sauce boils and thickens.

Add sour cream. Stir and heat through. Serve over or with Pork Schnitzel. Makes 2½ cups (675 mL).

POLYNESIAN HAM STEAK

Good, easy and a different way to prepare ham.

Cooking oil	1 tbsp.	15 mL
Center slice of ham, 1 inch (2.5 cm) thick	1	1
Water	1/3 cup	75 mL
Soy sauce	1/3 cup	75 mL
Sherry (or apple juice)	4 tbsp.	60 mL
Sliced green onion	1/3 cup	75 mL
Dry onion flakes	2 tsp.	10 mL
Ginger	1/4 tsp.	1 mL

Heat oil in frying pan. Add ham. Brown lightly on both sides.

Mix remaining ingredients together. Pour over ham. Simmer, turning often, for about 10 minutes. Serves 6.

CROWN ROAST OF PORK

A real showpiece. Serve with warm, chunky applesauce.

Crown roast of pork	**6 lbs.**	**2.75 kg**
Apple Stuffing, see page 149		

Place meat in roaster, bone ends down. Bake covered or uncovered in 325°F (160°C) oven for about 3 hours until the thermometer reads 170°F (78°C).

After meat has cooked for 2 hours, turn and put bone ends up. Put sleeve of foil in center. Fill center with stuffing. Cover stuffing with foil. Continue to cook until done. Serves 4 to 5.

GRAVY		
Pan drippings	6 tbsp.	100 mL
All-purpose flour	6 tbsp.	100 mL
Salt	3/4 tsp.	3 mL
Pepper	1/4 tsp.	1 mL
Water	3 cups	750 mL

Mix drippings, flour, salt and pepper in medium size saucepan. Add water. Heat and stir until it boils and thickens. If too pale, add a bit of gravy browner. Makes 3 cups (750 mL).

ORANGE SPARERIBS

A picture that you can eat.

Spareribs, cut serving size	4 lbs.	1.8 kg
Salt, sprinkle		
Pepper, sprinkle		
Frozen concentrated orange juice	½ × 6 oz.	½ × 170 g
Water	1 cup	225 mL
Granulated sugar	⅓ cup	75 mL
Cornstarch	2 tbsp.	30 mL
Lemon juice	2 tsp.	10 mL

Put ribs meaty side down in roaster. Sprinkle with salt and pepper. Cover. Roast in 350°F (180°C) oven for 30 minutes. Turn ribs and continue to roast for 30 minutes more. Drain off fat.

Mix remaining ingredients together in saucepan. Heat and stir over medium heat until it boils and thickens. Brush over ribs. Bake uncovered until tender about 30 to 40 minutes. Brush with sauce every 10 minutes. Garnish with slivered orange peel. Serve leftover sauce on the side. Serves 6.

SLIVERED ORANGE PEEL: Peel orange very thinly with no white pith on rind. Sliver with knife. Boil for 5 minutes with 1 cup (250 mL) water and ¼ cup (60 mL) granulated sugar. Drain.

Pictured on page 35.

SPICED HAM STEAK

Forms a lemon colored sauce. Nice tang.

Ham steaks, single serving size	4	4
Brown sugar, packed	⅓ cup	75 mL
Water	⅓ cup	75 mL
Vinegar	¼ cup	60 mL
Prepared mustard	2 tbsp.	30 mL
Salt	½ tsp.	2 mL

Place ham in baking dish.

Mix remaining ingredients together. Spoon over ham. Cover. Bake in 425°F (220°C) oven for about 20 to 30 minutes until sauce is bubbly and ham is cooked. Serves 4.

HAM STEAK

These ham steaks are topped with glazed sliced pineapple rings and cherries for added color.

Ham steaks, 4 - 6 oz. (112 - 168 g) each	8	8
Margarine (butter browns too fast)	2 tbsp.	30 mL
Canned pineapple slices, drained, reserve juice	8	8
Brown sugar	½ cup	125 mL
Cinnamon	¼ tsp.	1 mL
Reserved pineapple juice	1½ tbsp.	25 mL
Maraschino cherries, drained	8	8

Brown ham steaks lightly in margarine in frying pan or broil if you would rather. Keep hot.

Place pineapple slices in frying pan. Add sugar, cinnamon and pineapple juice. Turn so both sides are coated. Heat until bubbly and sugar is dissolved. If cooked too long, coating will harden. Arrange pineapple slices on ham steaks. Place cherry in center of each pineapple slice. Serves 8.

HAM AND PORK BAKE

Tasty and moist. Feed a crowd or use part and freeze the rest. Easy.

Ground ham	1½ lbs.	675 g
Ground fresh pork	1½ lbs.	675 g
Eggs, fork beaten	2	2
Milk	1 cup	250 mL
Lightly crushed corn flakes (or dry bread crumbs)	1 cup	250 mL
Pepper	¼ tsp.	1 mL

In large bowl mix all ingredients together well. Pack into 9 × 13 inch (22 × 33 cm) pan. Bake uncovered in 350°F (180°C) oven for 1 hour. Serve with Mustard Sauce (page 42). Serves 10 to 12.

CANNED HAM ROAST

Canned cherries make a fast sauce for the canned ham. Good shelfmates.

Canned ham	1½ lbs.	680 g
Whole cloves	14	14
Liquid honey	¼ cup	60 mL
Sour pitted cherries with juice	14 oz.	398 mL
Cornstarch	1 tbsp.	15 mL
Granulated sugar	¼ cup	60 mL
Allspice	¼ tsp.	1 mL
Cinnamon	¼ tsp.	1 mL

Put ham into casserole. Stick cloves in ham. Drizzle honey on top. Bake covered in 325°F (160°C) oven for about 1 hour.

Combine remaining ingredients in saucepan. Stir to dissolve cornstarch. Heat and stir until it boils and thickens. Slice ham onto platter. Spoon sauce over top or serve separately. Serves 4 to 5.

Variation: Omit cherries, cornstarch and sugar. Heat cherry pie filling, about 2 cups (500 mL) and add allspice and cinnamon.

CANDIED HAM

Dress up canned ham slices or ham steaks. Serve with Mustard Sauce, see page 42.

Canned ham, sliced	1½ lbs.	680 g
Brown sugar, packed	¾ cup	175 mL
Mustard powder	1 tbsp.	15 mL
Frozen condensed orange juice (or water)	4 tsp.	25 mL

Arrange ham slices in frying pan.

Mix remaining ingredients together. Spoon over ham. Fry slowly, turning often. Serves 4 to 5.

CANDIED HAM ROAST: Place whole ham in casserole. Cover with remaining ingredients. Bake uncovered in 325°F (160°C) oven for 30 minutes. Baste and continue to bake for about 30 more minutes. Baste often during this time. Serves 4 to 5.

FRANKFURTER STEW

Jazz up wieners with onion and tomatoes for a good flavor.

Chunked, chopped or sliced onion	2 cups	500 mL
Green pepper, chopped	1	1
Butter or margarine	3 tbsp.	50 mL
All-purpose flour	2 tbsp.	30 mL
Canned stewed tomatoes	2 × 14 oz.	2 × 398 mL
Wieners (10 - 12), cut bite size	1 lb.	450 g
Granulated sugar	2 tsp.	10 mL
Salt	½ tsp.	2 mL
Pepper	¼ tsp.	1 mL

Sauté onion and green pepper in butter in frying pan until soft.

Mix in flour. Stir in tomatoes until it boils and thickens.

Add remaining ingredients. Stir. Cover and simmer slowly to blend flavors and to heat through. Serves 4 to 5.

Pictured on page 53.

BAKED HAM

This appetizing glaze is ideal for ham steaks as well as a ham.

Ham, bone in, approximate weight	7 lbs.	3.2 kg
Whole cloves		
Brown sugar, packed	1 cup	250 mL
Soft honey	½ cup	125 mL

Using sharp knife score rind in diamond shape pattern about ¼ inch (6 mm) deep. Put ham into roaster. Cover. Bake in 350°F (180°C) oven for 2 hours. Remove from oven. Cut off rind in thin layer.

Stick whole clove into each diamond shape. Increase oven heat to 450°F (230°C).

Mix sugar with honey until smooth. Brush over ham. Bake uncovered, brushing with glaze again after 8 minutes until well glazed, about 15 minutes. Serve with Mustard Sauce (page 42). Serves 10.

Note: A ready to serve ham is used in this recipe. Internal temperature should read 140°F (60°C) when baked. Other hams should reach an internal temperature of 160°F (70°C).

HAM GLAZE WITH CLOVES

Brown sugar, packed	½ cup	125 mL
Cornstarch	1 tsp.	5 mL
Vinegar	¼ cup	60 mL
Prepared mustard	1 tsp.	5 mL
Cloves	⅛ tsp.	0.5 mL

Combine ingredients in saucepan. Mix well. Bring to a boil, stirring over medium heat. Smooth over your favorite ham loaf before baking. Super taste.

ORANGE HAM GLAZE

Brown sugar, packed	½ cup	125 mL
Prepared mustard	1 tbsp.	15 mL
Frozen concentrated orange juice	2 tbsp.	30 mL

Mix ingredients together and use as an alternative for topping ham loaves before baking.

CRANBERRY HAM GLAZE

Whole cranberry sauce	14 oz.	398 mL
Brown sugar	2 tbsp.	30 mL
Prepared mustard	2 tsp.	10 mL

Mix ingredients together well. Makes enough to cover 2 ham loaves before baking.

HAM WITH CRANBERRY: Spread whole cranberry sauce over ham loaf before baking. Mild flavor.

WIENER ROAST

Do something different with wieners. Roast them in a tasty mixture.

Envelope dry onion soup	1	1
Ketchup	⅓ cup	75 mL
Water	⅓ cup	75 mL
Brown sugar	2 tbsp.	30 mL
Prepared mustard	1 tbsp.	15 mL
Wieners, cut bite size	1 lb.	454 g

Mix ingredients together in order given. Put into 2 quart (2L) casserole. Roast uncovered in 350°F (180°C) oven for 45 to 60 minutes. Stir half way through baking. Serves 4.

MEDALLIONS OF PORK

For that very special dinner. Sure to impress.

Pork tenderloin	10 oz.	284 g
Margarine (butter browns too fast)	2 tbsp.	30 mL
Red pepper, cut in strips	1	1
Fresh mushrooms, sliced	3 - 10	3 - 10
Cornstarch	2 tsp.	10 mL
Water	½ cup	125 mL
Salt	¼ tsp.	1 mL
Pepper, sprinkle		
White wine (optional)	2 tsp.	10 mL

Cut pork tenderloin into 6 equal pieces and flatten to ¼ inch (6 mm) thickness. Sauté meat in margarine in frying pan until browned and no pink remains. Arrange meat on 2 plates.

Sauté pepper strips and sliced mushroom. Arrange around and on meat. Keep hot in oven.

Mix cornstarch in water. Pour into drippings in pan. Stir until boiling. Add salt, pepper and wine. Spoon a little over meat before serving. Serve with remaining sauce in small pitcher. Serves 2.

GOLDEN GLAZED CHICKEN

So attractive and it glistens. Very tasty.

Honey, liquid or softened	¼ cup	60 mL
Prepared mustard	¼ cup	60 mL
Tarragon	1 tsp.	5 mL
Chicken pieces	8	8

Mix honey, mustard and tarragon together.

Arrange chicken in single layer in small roaster. Spoon sauce over top being sure to put some on every piece. Bake uncovered in 350°F (180°C) oven until tender, about 1 hour. Place chicken on warm platter. Spoon sauce over to glaze. Serves 3 to 4.

Pictured on cover.

QUICK CHICK

A very simple and good chicken dish with two variations that are a must to try. Easy to double.

Chicken pieces	**3 lbs.**	**1.35 kg**
SAUCE		
Russian dressing	**½ cup**	**125 mL**
Apricot jam	**½ cup**	**125 mL**
Envelope dry onion soup	**1**	**1**

Arrange chicken pieces in single layer, skin side up in baking pan.

Sauce: Mix remaining ingredients together. Spoon over chicken making sure to get some on every piece. Cover. Bake in 350°F (180°C) oven for 1 hour until tender. Serves 4.

QUICK CHICK CURRY: Mix in 2 tsp. (10 mL) curry powder with above sauce. Makes a tasty meal.

QUICK CHICK ORANGE: Use orange marmalade instead of apricot jam. Just delicious.

CREOLE CHICKEN

Simply make tomato sauce, pour over chicken and bake.

Chicken pieces	**3 lbs.**	**1.35 kg**
Butter or margarine	**2 tbsp.**	**30 mL**
Large onion, chopped	**1**	**1**
Green pepper, chopped	**1**	**1**
Condensed cream of mushroom soup	**10 oz.**	**284 mL**
Canned tomatoes, broken up	**1 cup**	**250 mL**
Chicken bouillon powder	**1 tsp.**	**5 mL**
Granulated sugar	**½ tsp.**	**2 mL**

Arrange chicken pieces in small roaster.

Melt butter in frying pan. Add onion and green pepper. Sauté until soft.

Add remaining ingredients. Stir. Pour over chicken. Cover. Bake in 350°F (180°C) oven for about 1¼ hours until tender. Serves 4.

ROAST TURKEY

Just meant for a crowd.

No Fuss Stuffing, see page 148, make 1½ times recipe		
Turkey	**15 lbs.**	**6.75 kg**

Pack body cavity loosely with stuffing. Skewer shut. Tie wings to body and legs to tail. Put into roaster. Cover. Roast in 400°F (200°C) oven for 30 minutes. Turn heat to 325°F (160°C). Continue to roast until meat thermometer inserted in thigh, without touching bone, reads 190°F (90°C). Inserted from side of bird into center of stuffing it should read 165°F (75°C). Turkey leg should move or twist easily. Remove cover for last 30 minutes of cooking to brown. Allow 5½ to 6 hours for roasting. Pass the Cranberry Sauce (page 132). Serves 20.

GRAVY

Fat from roaster	**1 cup**	**250 mL**
All-purpose flour	**1 cup**	**250 mL**
Salt	**1½ tsp.**	**7 mL**
Pepper	**¼ tsp.**	**1 mL**
Water (include drippings without fat)	**8 cups**	**2 L**

Remove turkey from roaster. Pour off drippings. Measure fat required and return to roaster. Mix in flour, salt and pepper. Add water and drippings. Heat and stir until it boils and thickens. Add a bit of gravy browner if needed. Taste for salt and pepper adding more as required. Use a wire whisk to make lump free gravy. Makes 8 cups (2 L).

SWEET AND SOUR CHICKEN

Baked in a tasty sauce. A good balance of flavors.

Chicken thighs and drumsticks, skin removed	**3 lbs.**	**1.35 kg**
Brown sugar, packed	**1 cup**	**250 mL**
Water	**1 cup**	**250 mL**
White vinegar	**½ cup**	**125 mL**
Ketchup	**2 tbsp.**	**30 mL**
Soy sauce	**1 tbsp.**	**15 mL**
Cornstarch	**3 tbsp.**	**45 mL**
Water	**2 tbsp.**	**30 mL**

(continued on next page)

Arrange chicken pieces in 3 quart (3.5 L) casserole.

Mix sugar, first amount of water, vinegar, ketchup and soy sauce together in saucepan over medium heat.

Mix cornstarch in remaining water. Stir into saucepan until it boils and thickens. Pour over chicken. Cover. Bake in 350°F (180°C) oven for about 1¼ hours until tender. Spoon sauce over chicken before serving. Serves 4 to 5.

CHICKEN PARISIÈNNE

Attractive, moist and tasty. Although chicken may be added without pre-browning, it does have a bit more flavor when browned first.

Large chicken breasts, halved, skin removed	**3**	**3**
Margarine (butter browns too fast)	**¼ cup**	**60 mL**
Salt, sprinkle		
Pepper, sprinkle		
Canned tiny onions, drained (see Note)	**14 oz.**	**398 mL**
Canned sliced mushrooms, drained	**10 oz.**	**284 mL**
Condensed cream of chicken soup	**10 oz.**	**284 mL**
Apple juice	**¼ cup**	**60 mL**
Thyme	**⅛ tsp.**	**0.5 mL**
Paprika, good sprinkle		

Brown chicken breasts in margarine in frying pan. Sprinkle with salt and pepper. Transfer to small roaster.

Spread onions and mushrooms over chicken.

Mix soup, apple juice and thyme together. Spoon over top.

Sprinkle with paprika. Cover. Bake in 350°F (180°C) oven for about 1 hour or until tender when pierced with fork. Serves 6.

Note: If you cannot find canned onions, substitute 1½ cups (375 mL) cooked whole pearl onions or cut-up onions, cooked.

Paré Pointer

If you think twice before you say anything, you won't even get in on the conversation.

FAST CHICKEN

No pre-browning of chicken. Try the variation as well. Makes a yummy gravy. A good company dish.

Chicken breasts, halved	6	6
Condensed cream of mushroom soup	10 oz.	284 mL
Sour cream	1 cup	250 mL
Envelope dry onion soup	1	1
Lemon juice	1 tbsp.	15 mL
Dill seed (optional)	1 tsp.	5 mL
Salt	1 tsp.	5 mL
Pepper	¼ tsp.	1 mL
Paprika, good sprinkle		
Chow mein noodles	1 cup	250 mL

Put chicken into small roaster or large baking dish.

Mix the next 7 ingredients well. Pour over chicken.

Sprinkle with paprika. Scatter noodles over all. Cover. Bake in 350°F (180°C) oven for about 1 to 1½ hours until tender. Serves 12.

Variation: Omit dill seed. Sprinkle with dill weed before baking. A pleasant flavor.

FAST COMPANY CHICKEN: Add 14 oz. (398 mL) can of tiny onions, drained (see Note) and 10 oz. (284 mL) can of whole or sliced mushrooms, drained. More special than the great Fast Chicken.

Note: If you cannot find canned onions, substitute 1½ cups (375 mL) cooked whole pearl onions or cut up onions, cooked.

Paré Pointer

Mrs. Mouse wants to move again. She gets so tired of living in a hole in the wall.

CHICKEN PARMESAN

Tasty and quick to prepare. The addition of oregano gives a faint comparison to the flavor of pizza.

Fine dry bread crumbs	½ cup	125 mL
Grated Parmesan cheese	¾ cup	175 mL
Salt	1 tsp.	5 mL
Pepper	¼ tsp.	1 mL
Garlic powder	¼ tsp.	1 mL
Oregano (optional)	½ tsp.	2 mL
Whole chicken, cut up	3 lbs.	1.35 kg
(or use all chicken breasts)		
Butter or margarine, melted	½ cup	125 mL

Mix first 6 ingredients together in small bowl.

Dip chicken into melted butter then into dry mixture to coat. Arrange in baking pan. Cover. Bake in 350°F (180°C) oven until tender, about 1 to 1¼ hours. Serves 3 to 4.

SAUCY CHICKEN

This simple quick dish has a mild barbecued flavor.

Ketchup	½ cup	125 mL
Brown sugar, packed	¼ cup	60 mL
Vinegar	¼ cup	60 mL
Worcestershire sauce	2 tsp.	10 mL
Onion powder	½ tsp.	2 mL
Garlic powder	½ tsp.	2 mL
Salt	2 tsp.	10 mL
Pepper	½ tsp.	2 mL
Chicken pieces	3 lbs.	1.35 kg

Mix first 8 ingredients together in small bowl.

Arrange chicken in baking pan or casserole large enough for single layer. Pour sauce over top being sure to get some on every piece. Cover. Bake in 350°F (180°C) oven until tender, about 1 to 1¼ hours. Serves 3 to 4.

BARBECUE SAUCED WINGS

Although many ingredients go into this sauce, it is easy to make. Lots of flavor.

Chicken wings	3 lbs.	1.35 kg

BARBECUE SAUCE

Ketchup	¼ cup	60 mL
Water	¼ cup	60 mL
Brown sugar, packed	¼ cup	60 mL
Vinegar	¼ cup	60 mL
Worcestershire sauce	2 tbsp.	30 mL
Cooking oil	2 tbsp.	30 mL
Prepared mustard	1 tsp.	5 mL
Paprika	1 tsp.	5 mL
Salt	1 tsp.	5 mL
Pepper	¼ tsp.	1 mL
Dry onion flakes	1 tbsp.	15 mL

Cut off chicken wing tips and discard.

Barbecue Sauce: Mix all 11 ingredients together in saucepan. Simmer 5 minutes.

Brush each piece of chicken with sauce. Arrange in single layer on greased or foil lined baking sheet. Spoon sauce over wings. Bake uncovered in 350°F (180°C) oven until tender, about 30 to 40 minutes. Serves 3 about 6 wings each.

Pictured on page 71.

CHICKEN IN CREAM

A simple and delicious Ukrainian recipe.

Whole chicken, cut up (or parts)	2½ - 3 lbs.	1.1 - 1.3 kg
Margarine (butter browns too fast)	2 - 4 tbsp.	30 - 60 mL
Medium onion, sliced	1	1
Heavy cream	1½ cups	375 mL

Brown chicken in margarine in large frying pan. Remove onto plate.

Add onion and sauté until soft. Add more margarine if needed. Add chicken.

Pour heavy cream over top. Cover. Barely simmer for 20 to 30 minutes until tender. Serves 3 to 4.

WINGS PARMESAN

These have a crispy, delectable coating. Sure to disappear in a hurry.

Grated Parmesan cheese	¾ **cup**	**175 mL**
Fine dry bread crumbs	¼ **cup**	**60 mL**
Paprika	**1 tsp.**	**5 mL**
Salt	**1 tsp.**	**5 mL**
Pepper	¼ **tsp.**	**1 mL**
Oregano	¼ **tsp.**	**1 mL**
Thyme	¼ **tsp.**	**1 mL**
Chicken wings	**2 lbs.**	**900 g**
Butter or margarine, melted	½ **cup**	**125 mL**

Mix first 7 ingredients together.

Cut off chicken wing tips and discard. Dip wings into melted butter then coat with dry mixture. Arrange on greased, foil lined baking sheet. Bake in 350°F (180°C) oven for 30 to 45 minutes until tender. Serves 2 about 6 wings each.

Pictured on page 89.

CHICKEN NUGGETS

Very tasty little things and so convenient to cook them in the oven.

Boneless chicken breasts, halved, skin removed	**2 lbs.**	**900 mL**
Envelope dry onion soup	**1**	**1**
Fine dry bread crumbs	½ **cup**	**125 mL**
Butter or margarine, melted	¼ **cup**	**60 mL**

Cut meat into 1 inch (2.5 cm) squares.

Mix onion soup with bread crumbs. Coat damp chicken pieces well. Place on greased baking sheet. Sprinkle remaining crumb mixture over top.

Drizzle melted butter over top. Bake in 400°F (200°C) oven for 10 minutes. Turn over and bake another 10 minutes. Serve with Barbecue Sauce (page 122), Sweet And Sour Sauce (page 66), or ketchup. Serves 4 to 5.

Pictured on page 71.

CURRIED CHICKEN

Excellent flavor with a good nip.

Chicken thighs and drumsticks	2 lbs.	900 g
Lemon juice	3 tbsp.	50 mL
Worcestershire sauce	2 tbsp.	30 mL
Curry powder	1 tbsp.	15 mL
Paprika	1 tsp.	5 mL
Salt	1½ tsp.	7 mL
Pepper	½ tsp.	2 mL
Butter or margarine	2 tbsp.	30 mL
Brown sugar	1 tbsp.	15 mL
Medium onion, chopped	1	1
Large tomato, chopped	1	1

Pat chicken dry with paper towels.

Mix next 6 ingredients together. Brush over chicken. Cover and let stand in refrigerator for 3 hours.

Melt butter and sugar in frying pan. Add chicken and brown slowly.

Add onion and tomato. Cover. Simmer slowly until chicken is tender, about 35 minutes. Serves 3 to 4.

MUSHROOM CHICKEN

This is it — the easiest meat dish there is. It takes about two minutes to put this into the oven.

Whole chicken, cut up	2½ lbs.	1.2 kg
Condensed cream of mushroom soup	10 oz.	284 mL
Envelope dry onion soup	1	1

Place chicken in small roaster.

Spoon mushroom soup over top of chicken. Sprinkle with onion soup. Cover. Bake in 350°F (180°C) oven for about 1 to 1¼ hours or until tender. Serves 3.

Variation: To make this a bit more special, add 10 oz. (284 mL) canned sliced mushrooms, drained, before adding soups.

CHICKEN PACKETS

All done up for easy serving. Can be made ahead and baked when needed. Serve a side dish of stuffing if desired.

Boneless chicken breasts, halved, skin removed	2	2
Margarine (butter browns too fast)	2 tbsp.	30 mL
Chopped onion	½ cup	125 mL
Chopped fresh mushrooms	1¼ cups	300 mL
Margarine	2 tbsp.	30 mL
Frozen puff pastry, thawed	1 lb.	454 g

Fry chicken in first amount of margarine until cooked, about 15 minutes. Add more margarine if needed. Remove and cool.

Sauté onion and mushrooms in margarine until soft. Cool.

Roll out pastry on lightly floured surface. Lay 1 chicken piece on top. Spoon ¼ onion-mushroom mixture along one side. Dampen pastry around 1 side of meat. Fold over and seal. Cut this away from rest of pastry. Cut 2 to 3 slits in top. Place on ungreased baking sheet. Bake in 425°F (220°C) oven until browned, about 15 to 20 minutes. Serves 4.

CHICKEN BREASTS SUPREME

Marinated overnight, this is ready to crumb and chill a few hours before mealtime. Fabulous flavor.

Chicken breasts, halved, skin and bone removed	6	6
Sour cream	2 cups	500 mL
Lemon juice	1 tbsp.	15 mL
Worcestershire sauce	1 tbsp.	15 mL
Seasoned salt	1½ tsp.	7 mL
Paprika	1 tsp.	5 mL
Fine dry bread crumbs	1¾ cups	425 mL
Butter or margarine, melted	12 tbsp.	180 mL

Pat meat dry with paper towels.

Mix next 5 ingredients together in large bowl. Add chicken being sure to coat every piece. Cover. Chill overnight.

Remove chicken from sour cream mixture. Roll in crumbs, covering completely. Place on foil-lined or greased pan large enough to hold in single layer. Chill at least 2 hours before cooking.

When ready to cook, drizzle 1 tbsp. (15 mL) melted butter over each piece. Cook uncovered in 350°F (180°C) oven for about 1 hour until tender. Serves 8 to 10.

CHICKEN KIEV

The buttery center with parsley and chives spurts out when this delectable morsel is cut.

Large boneless chicken breasts, halved, skin removed	4	4
Butter or margarine, softened	½ cup	125 mL
Chopped parsley	2 tbsp.	30 mL
Chopped chives	1 tbsp.	15 mL
Eggs, beaten	2	2
Milk	2 tbsp.	30 mL
Fine dry bread crumbs	1 cup	250 mL
Fat for deep-frying		

(continued on next page)

Pound meat with mallet to ⅛ inch (4 mm) thickness. Cover with waxed paper or plastic before pounding so as not to make holes right through.

Mix butter, parsley and chives together. Chill. Shape into 8 balls with your fingers. Keep chilled.

Beat eggs and milk together.

Lay butter ball on meat. Fold meat over butter, pressing butter to fit, tucking in ends to cover well. Secure with wooden picks. Dip into egg then crumbs.

Deep-fry in 375°F (190°C) hot fat for about 15 to 20 minutes until golden. Remove picks to serve. Serves 8.

Pictured on page 125.

JAPANESE CHICKEN WINGS

Make lots of these appealing morsels. Dark and delicious.

Chicken wings	3 lbs.	1.35 kg
Soy sauce	½ cup	125 mL
Sake (or apple juice)	½ cup	125 mL
Granulated sugar	3 tbsp.	50 mL
Garlic powder	¼ tsp.	1 mL
Ginger	¼ tsp.	1 mL
Paprika	½ tsp.	2 mL
Chili powder	½ tsp.	2 mL

Remove chicken wing tips and discard. Arrange in greased pan large enough to hold in single layer.

Mix remaining 7 ingredients together. Spoon over chicken. Bake uncovered in 350°F (180°C) oven for 30 to 45 minutes until tender. Serves 3 about 6 wings each.

Paré Pointer

Gramma had wheels on her rocking chair 'cause she always wanted to rock and roll.

CHICKEN IN MUSHROOM SAUCE

Moist and flavorful.

Small chicken breasts	6	6
Margarine (butter browns too fast)	1/4 cup	50 mL
Salt, sprinkle		
Pepper, sprinkle		
Heavy cream	1 cup	250 mL
Paprika	1 tsp.	5 mL
Sliced mushrooms, drained	10 oz.	284 mL
Chives	2 tsp.	10 mL
White wine (or apple juice)	1/3 cup	75 mL

Brown chicken in margarine in frying pan. Sprinkle with salt and pepper during browning.

Add cream, paprika, mushrooms and chives. Cover. Simmer slowly for about 20 minutes until tender.

Add wine. Simmer 3 more minutes. Serves 6.

ROAST DUCK

Ducks can be bought in most supermarkets. Wonderful for those dark meat lovers. Great with applesauce.

Duck	4 1/2 lbs.	2 kg
Slice of onion	1	1
Stuffing Balls, see page 38		

Tie wings to body with string. Put onion slice n cavity. Tie legs together then to tail. Place in roaster. Cover. Bake in 450°F (230°C) oven for 15 minutes. Turn oven to 350°F (180°C). Continue to roast for 1 1/2 to 2 hours until tender. If you plan to carve at the dinner table and would like the duck to be browner, remove cover when tender and turn heat to 400°F (200°C) for a few minutes. Serves 4.

Gravy: Pour off most of the fat leaving 1/4 cup (60 mL) in pan. Mix in 1/4 cup (60 mL) all-purpose flour, 1/2 tsp. (2 mL) salt and 1/8 tsp. (0.5 mL) pepper. Add 2 cups (450 mL) water. Stir over medium heat until it boils and thickens. Taste for salt and pepper. Thin with water if needed. Makes 2 cups (450 mL).

(continued on next page)

Note: If making Stuffing Balls you will have some left over which can be frozen. If you would rather stuff the duck use No Fuss Stuffing (page 148). Make ½ recipe.

SPEEDY DUCK/SPEEDY CHICKEN: Cut into quarters or pieces. Place in roaster. Sprinkle with 1 envelope dry onion soup. Cover. Bake in 325°F (160°C) oven for about 1½ hours or until very tender. Quick and easy. White wine or apple juice, about ½ cup (125 mL) may be added if desired. Use 2 ducks at least 4 lbs. (2 kg) each or the same weight in chicken. Lining pan with foil makes for easy clean up.

CHICKEN WITH BACON

The bacon is cooked with the chicken but served with the extra flavorful gravy.

All-purpose flour	⅓ cup	75 mL
Salt	1 tsp.	5 mL
Pepper	¼ tsp.	1 mL
Thyme	¼ tsp.	1 mL
Large chicken breasts, halved	2	2
Bacon slices, diced	8	8
GRAVY		
Reserved flour mixture	2 tbsp.	30 mL
Chicken bouillon cubes	2 × ⅕ oz.	2 × 6 g
Boiling water	1½ cups	350 mL

Mix flour, salt, pepper and thyme together in paper or plastic bag.

Add two chicken pieces at a time. Shake to coat. Save flour that is left.

Put bacon into frying pan with floured chicken. Cook on low heat for 30 minutes. Turn and cook 30 minutes more until tender. Put cover askew on pan, not on tightly, while cooking. Transfer chicken to platter. Keep warm while making gravy. Serves 4.

Gravy: Add reserved flour mixture to very crisp bacon in frying pan. Stir until white color disappears. Add a bit of butter or margarine if necessary.

Dissolve bouillon cubes in boiling water. Stir into bacon-flour mixture until it boils and thickens. Loosen any bits on bottom of pan. Makes 3 cups (700 mL) crunchy gravy.

CHICKEN AND RICE

Just layer in a baking dish, cover and bake to have this tasty moist dish ready when you are.

Long grain rice	1½ cups	350 mL
Envelope dry onion soup	1	1
Chicken pieces	3 lbs.	1.35 kg
Condensed cream of mushroom soup	10 oz.	284 mL
Condensed cream of chicken soup	10 oz.	284 mL
Evaporated milk	13½ oz.	385 mL
Water or milk	1 cup	250 mL
Paprika, sprinkle		

Spread rice in 9 × 13 inch (22 × 33 cm) baking pan. Sprinkle dry soup over rice. Arrange chicken over top.

Mix both soups with evaporated milk and water. Pour over all.

Sprinkle with paprika. Cover. Bake in 350°F (180°C) oven for about 2 hours until rice and chicken are cooked. Serves 6.

ORANGE CRANBERRY SAUCE

A good blend of flavors. Try putting sauce through a food mill for a smooth texture.

Prepared orange juice	1 cup	250 mL
Granulated sugar	1 cup	250 mL
Cranberries, fresh or frozen	2 cups	500 mL

Bring orange juice and sugar to a boil in saucepan over medium heat.

Add cranberries. Cook until skins pop, about 5 minutes. Remove from heat. Sauce will thicken as it cools. Makes a generous 2 cups (500 mL).

CRANBERRY SAUCE: Use water instead of orange juice.

Paré Pointer

Yes, Rock Stars are cool. Look at how many fans they have.

CHICKEN CACCIATORE

A flavorful zesty meat. Simply brown chicken, add the rest of the ingredients and simmer until done.

All-purpose flour	1/3 cup	75 mL
Salt	1 tsp.	5 mL
Pepper	1/4 tsp.	1 mL
Chicken pieces	3 lbs.	1.35 kg
Margarine (butter browns too fast)	1/4 cup	60 mL
Chopped onion	1 cup	250 mL
Small green pepper, chopped	1	1
Sliced mushrooms, drained	10 oz.	284 mL
Tomato sauce	7½ oz.	213 mL
Canned tomatoes	14 oz.	398 mL
Bay leaf	1	1
Oregano	½ tsp.	2 mL
Garlic powder	1/4 tsp.	1 mL
Granulated sugar	1 tsp.	5 mL
Thyme	1/4 tsp.	1 mL
Basil	1/4 tsp.	1 mL

Grated Parmesan cheese, sprinkle

Combine flour, salt and pepper in paper or plastic bag.

Put 2 or 3 chicken pieces into bag at a time. Shake to coat. Brown in margarine in frying pan or large heavy Dutch oven. Remove chicken as it is browned.

Add onion and green pepper to pan. Sauté until soft. Add more margarine if needed.

Measure in next 9 ingredients. Stir.

Add chicken. Sprinkle with grated Parmesan cheese. Cover. Simmer slowly for about 35 to 40 minutes until tender. Serves 4 to 5.

Pictured on page 53.

Paré Pointer

A giraffe is slow in apologizing. It takes a long time to swallow its pride.

FRIED CHICKEN

Brown chicken in the morning or even the day before. It finishes cooking in the oven with no further attention. The gravy is a bonus.

Large chicken breasts	4	4
Chicken thighs	6	6
All-purpose flour	²/₃ cup	150 mL
Salt	2 tsp.	10 mL
Pepper	¼ tsp.	1 mL
Paprika	2 tsp.	10 mL
Margarine (butter browns too fast)	2 tbsp.	30 mL

Have the butcher cut breasts into 3 pieces each or if you have a cleaver or hatchet you can cut them at home. Protect your bread board with cardboard to prevent gouging.

Combine flour, salt, pepper and paprika in paper or plastic bag. Mix. Place 3 or 4 chicken pieces in bag. Shake to coat.

Brown in frying pan in margarine adding more margarine as needed. May be chilled in small roaster at this point. To cook, put covered roaster in 350°F (180°C) oven for about 1 to 1½ hours until tender. Serves 8.

FRIED CHICKEN IN GRAVY

All-purpose flour	½ cup	125 mL
Butter or margarine, as needed	¼ - ½ cup	50-125 mL
Salt	1½ tsp.	7 mL
Pepper	¼ tsp.	1 mL
Water	6 cups	1.35 L

Stir flour into any remaining fat in pan along with smaller amount of butter. Add more butter as needed to moisten flour. Mix in salt and pepper. Stir in water until it boils. Loosen all bits from bottom of pan. Gravy will be thin. Pour over chicken in roaster. Bake covered in 350°F (180°C) oven for about 1 to 1½ hours, until tender when pierced with fork.

Note: To serve gravy on the side use only 4 cups (900 mL) water and 1 tsp. (5 mL) salt.

A layer of stuffing with a layer of chicken cooked worry-free in the oven. Top it with a thick mushroom sauce. Sure to please.

Dry bread crumbs or cubes	2 cups	500 mL
Chopped celery	½ cup	125 mL
Finely chopped onion	½ cup	125 mL
Poultry seasoning	¾ tsp.	4 mL
Parsley flakes	½ tsp.	2 mL
Salt	½ tsp.	2 mL
Pepper	⅛ tsp.	0.5 mL
Chicken bouillon cubes	2 × ⅕ oz.	2 × 6 g
Boiling water	2 cups	500 mL
Large chicken breasts, halved, skin removed	3	3
Salt, sprinkle		
Pepper, sprinkle		
Paprika, good sprinkle		

Mix first 7 ingredients together in 9 × 13 inch (22 × 33 cm) baking pan.

Dissolve bouillon cubes in boiling water. Add to crumb mixture. Mix well.

Arrange chicken over top. Sprinkle with salt, pepper and paprika. Bake uncovered in 325°F (160°C) oven for 30 minutes. Cover. Continue to bake for 30 to 45 minutes more until tender. Spoon Mushroom Sauce over chicken. Serves 6.

MUSHROOM SAUCE

Butter or margarine	3 tbsp.	50 mL
Chopped onion	½ cup	125 mL
Chopped fresh mushrooms	2 cups	500 mL
All-purpose flour	2 tbsp.	30 mL
Salt	½ tsp.	2 mL
Pepper	⅛ tsp.	0.5 mL
Cream or milk	1 cup	250 mL

Melt butter in frying pan. Add onion. Sauté for 2 to 3 minutes then add mushrooms. Sauté until onion is soft and clear.

Mix in flour, salt and pepper. Stir in cream until it boils and thickens. It will be fairly thick. If you would rather have a thinner sauce, add a little more cream. Spoon over chicken and stuffing. Makes a generous 2 cups (500mL).

ROCK CORNISH HENS

These little beauties make any meal festive.

Cornish hens, about 1 lb. (500 g) each	**6**	**6**
Wild Rice Stuffing, see below		
Paprika, sprinkle		

Stuff birds. Skewer closed. Tie wings to body. Tie legs to body and tail. Sprinkle with paprika. Arrange in large roaster. Roast uncovered in 400°F (200°C) oven for about 1 hour until tender. After roasting ½ hour, brush with melted butter. Sprinkle with more paprika if desired. Serves 6.

WILD RICE STUFFING

Long grain and wild rice mix	**6 oz.**	**200 g**
Salted water		
Chopped onion	**1 cup**	**250 mL**
Chopped celery	**½ cup**	**125 mL**
Finely grated carrot	**½ cup**	**125 mL**
Butter or margarine	**¼ cup**	**60 mL**
Fresh mushrooms, chopped	**1⅓ cups**	**325 mL**
Salt	**½ tsp.**	**2 mL**
Pepper	**⅛ tsp.**	**0.5 mL**
Poultry seasoning	**½ tsp.**	**2 mL**

Cook rice according to package directions.

Sauté onion, celery and carrot in butter in frying pan until soft.

Add mushrooms, salt, pepper and poultry seasoning. Sauté about 2 minutes more. Add to rice. Mix well. Stuff hens.

Paré Pointer

Don't you sometimes wonder about parents? They put their children to bed when they're wide awake and get them up when they're sleepy.

Serve this with warm fresh applesauce for a special treat.

Goose	10 lbs.	4.5 kg
Potato Stuffing, see below		

Pull away as much fat as you can from cavity and discard.

Stuff goose. Skewer shut. Tie wings to body and legs to tail. Place in roaster. Roast uncovered in 450°F (230°) oven for 30 minutes. Prick skin and allow fat to run out. Drain off fat. Cover. Lower heat to 350°F (180°C). Roast until tender, about 3½ to 4 hours or until meat thermometer reaches 190°F (87°C). If not brown enough, remove cover for a few minutes. Serves 10.

POTATO STUFFING

Mashed potato	3 cups	750 mL
Dry bread crumbs	3 cups	750 mL
Parsley flakes	2 tsp.	10 mL
Sage	1½ tsp.	7 mL
Salt	¾ tsp.	4 mL
Pepper	¼ tsp.	1 mL
Water		
Chopped onion	1 cup	250 mL
Butter or margarine	¼ cup	60 mL

Mix first 6 ingredients together in large bowl. Add water as needed to make stuffing damp.

Sauté onion in butter in frying pan until soft. Mix in with potato mixture. Makes 7 cups (1.5 L) stuffing.

GRAVY

Fat drippings from pan	¾ cup	175 mL
All-purpose flour	¾ cup	175 mL
Salt	1 tsp.	5 mL
Pepper	¼ tsp.	1 mL
Pan drippings, without fat, plus water if needed	6 cups	1.5 L

Mix fat, flour, salt and pepper together in large saucepan. Stir in drippings and water until it boils and thickens. Add a bit of gravy browner if needed. Makes 6 cups (1.5 L).

CHICKEN LOAF

Not your usual beef meatloaf. This one is served sliced and sauced.

Chicken thighs (or use 4 lbs., 1.8 kg, chicken or hen, cut up)	3 lbs.	1.35 kg
Water	3 cups	700 mL
Celery flakes	1 tsp.	5 mL
Parsley flakes	1 tsp.	5 mL
Salt	1 tsp.	5 mL
Eggs	4	4
Milk	1 cup	225 mL
Chicken broth, reserved	2 cups	450 mL
Dry bread crumbs	1²/₃ cup	375 mL
Poultry seasoning	1 tsp.	5 mL
Paprika	1 tsp.	5 mL
Salt	1 tsp.	5 mL
Diced cooked chicken	4 cups	900 mL

First prepare chicken. Put thighs, water, celery flakes, parsley and salt into large saucepan. Cover. Boil until tender. Remove chicken. Reserve broth. Remove meat from bones. Dice finely for easy slicing of finished loaf. You should have 4 cups (900 mL) of meat.

Beat eggs in bowl until frothy. Add remaining ingredients. Stir. Pack into greased 9 × 5 × 3 inch (23 × 12 × 7 cm) loaf pan. Bake in 350°F (180°C) oven for 1 to 1½ hours. Loaf will test done when an inserted knife comes out clean. Serve in slices with Mushroom Sauce spooned over top. Serves 6.

MUSHROOM SAUCE

Butter or margarine	¼ cup	60 mL
All-purpose flour	¼ cup	60 mL
Salt	½ tsp.	2 mL
Pepper	⅛ tsp.	0.5 mL
Parsley flakes	1 tsp.	5 mL
Chicken bouillon powder	4 tsp.	20 mL
Worcestershire sauce	½ tsp.	2 mL
Paprika	½ tsp.	2 mL
Water	2 cups	450 mL
Sliced mushrooms, drained	½ cup	125 mL

Melt butter in saucepan over medium heat. Mix in flour, salt, pepper, parsley, bouillon powder, Worcestershire sauce and paprika. Stir in water and mushrooms until it boils and thickens. Spoon over sliced Chicken Loaf or Stuffed Meatloaf (page 79). Makes 2 cups (450 mL).

CHICKEN FLORENTINE SANDWICH

Very little effort produces this gourmet dish.

Small chicken breasts, halved, skin removed, boned	6	6
Grated Parmesan cheese	½ cup	125 mL
Frozen spinach, cooked and drained	10 oz.	300 g
Egg	1	1
All-purpose flour	1 tsp.	5 mL
Salt	¾ tsp.	4 mL
Pepper	¼ tsp.	1 mL
Nutmeg	¼ tsp.	1 mL
Cooked ham, thin slices	6	6
Egg	1	1
Water	2 tbsp.	30 mL
Fine dry bread crumbs	1 cup	250 mL
Butter or margarine, melted	⅓ cup	75 mL

Pound chicken flat with meat mallet. Lay all 12 pieces on counter. Sprinkle cheese on 6 pieces.

Combine spinach, first egg, flour, salt, pepper and nutmeg in blender. Purée. Put spoonful on each of the 6 pieces over cheese.

Cut ham to fit and place over spinach mixture. Lay remaining 6 chicken pieces over all. Pinch edges together.

Beat second egg and water with fork to make egg wash.

Dip chicken sandwiches into egg wash then coat with crumbs. Arrange in well greased baking pan large enough to hold in single layer. Drizzle with melted butter. Bake in 400°F (200°C) oven for about 30 to 40 minutes until browned and cooked. Turn at half time for more even browning. Serves 6.

Pictured on page 89.

Pare Pointer

Hay and a mouse are quite similar. The catt'le eat it.

CHICKEN CORDON BLEU

Three choices for this classic. Bake in a mushroom sauce, pan-fry or crumb and bake in the oven.

Large boneless chicken breasts, halved	3	3
Salt, sprinkle		
Cooked ham slices, thin	6	6
Swiss cheese	6 oz.	170 g
All-purpose flour	¼ cup	60 mL
Margarine (butter browns too fast)	2 tbsp.	30 mL
Chicken bouillon cubes	3 × ⅕ oz.	3 × 6 g
Boiling water	½ cup	125 mL
Sliced mushrooms, drained	10 oz.	284 mL
White wine (or apple juice)	⅓ cup	75 mL
All-purpose flour	2 tbsp.	30 mL
Water	½ cup	125 mL
Toasted almonds	½ cup	125 mL

Pound chicken flat with mallet to ¼ inch (6 mm) thickness. Sprinkle with salt.

Lay ham slice over top. Cut cheese into 6 equal sticks. Lay stick over ham. Roll like jelly roll, tucking sides in. Skewer or tie.

Coat rolls in first amount of flour. Let stand 20 minutes. Brown in margarine in frying pan. Add more margarine as needed. Transfer to baking dish large enough to fit in single layer.

In same frying pan dissolve bouillon cubes in first amount of water. Add mushrooms and wine. Pour over chicken scraping all bits stuck to pan. Cover. Bake in 350°F (180°C) oven for 1 to 1½ hours until tender. Remove rolls to hot platter.

Mix remaining flour and water together until no lumps remain. Stir into liquid in baking pan over medium heat until it boils and thickens.

Pour over chicken and garnish with almonds that have been toasted in 350°F (180°C) oven until browned, about 5 minutes. Stir twice. Serves 6.

PAN CORDON BLEU: Chicken rolls may be fried until cooked through.

(continued on next page)

OVEN CORDON BLEU: After rolling tightly, dip bottom of chicken into melted butter then into fine dry bread crumbs. Place into baking pan. Brush with melted butter. Sprinkle with crumbs. Cover. Bake in 350°F (180°C) oven for 45 minutes. Remove cover. Continue to bake for about 30 minutes more until golden brown.

COQ AU VIN

For those who don't cook with wine, alcohol-free wine gives this dish an authentic flavor.

Margarine (butter browns too fast)	¼ cup	60 mL
Large chicken breasts, halved, skin removed	4	4
Chopped onion	½ cup	125 mL
Salt, sprinkle		
Pepper, sprinkle		
Bacon slices, diced	6	6
Tiny onions, peeled	12 - 20	12 - 20
Small mushrooms	½ lb.	225 g
Garlic clove, crushed	1	1
All-purpose flour	1 tbsp.	15 mL
Red wine	1 cup	250 mL
Parsley sprigs	2	2
Small bay leaf	1	1
Thyme	¼ tsp.	1 mL

Melt margarine in frying pan. Brown chicken and sauté onion until soft and clear. Sprinkle with salt and pepper. Transfer to small roaster.

Put bacon, onions, mushrooms and garlic into frying pan. Sauté until bacon is cooked.

Mix in flour. Stir in wine until it boils and thickens slightly. Add parsley, bay leaf and thyme. Turn into small roaster. Cover. Bake in 325°F (160°C) oven until tender, about 1 hour. This may also be simmered slowly on top of the stove for about the same time. Discard bay leaf. Serves 8.

Paré Pointer

They thought Scotch eggs came from drunk chickens.

TARRAGON CHICKEN

If you don't have this spice on hand, it may be baked without for an equally tasty meat. Tarragon adds an interesting flavor to the chicken.

Chicken breasts, halved (boneless is best)	**4**	**4**
Condensed cream of mushroom soup	**10 oz.**	**284 mL**
Sour cream	**1 cup**	**225 mL**
Sherry (or apple juice)	**¼ cup**	**50 mL**
Fresh mushrooms, sliced or left whole (optional)	**1½ cups**	**375 mL**
Salt	**½ tsp.**	**2 mL**
Pepper	**⅛ tsp.**	**0.5 mL**
Tarragon	**1 tsp.**	**5 mL**
Sliced almonds	**¼ cup**	**50 mL**

Place chicken in small roaster.

Mix next 7 ingredients together. Spread over chicken.

Sprinkle with almonds. Cover. Bake in 350°F (180°C) oven for about 1½ hours until tender. Serves 6 to 8.

1. Ham Tomato Loaf page 88
2. Corned Beef Balls page 82
3. Stuffing Balls page 38
4. Veal Roast page 80

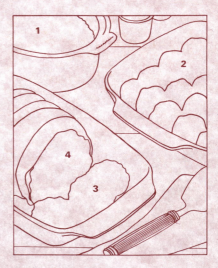

CHICKEN IN WINE

Great flavor with lots of gravy.

All-purpose flour	½ cup	125 mL
Salt	1 tsp.	5 mL
Pepper	¼ tsp.	1 mL
Whole chicken, cut up	4 lbs.	1.8 kg
Margarine (butter browns too fast)	¼ cup	60 mL
Sliced fresh mushrooms	2 cups	500 mL
Condensed cream of mushroom soup	10 oz.	284 mL
Chicken broth	½ cup	125 mL
Prepared orange juice	½ cup	125 mL
Dry white wine (or use apple juice)	½ cup	125 mL
Brown sugar	1 tbsp.	15 mL
Medium carrots, cut in matchsticks	4	4

Mix flour, salt and pepper together in paper or plastic bag.

Add chicken, a few pieces at a time and shake to coat. Brown in margarine in frying pan. Transfer to small roaster.

Sauté mushrooms until soft, adding more margarine if needed.

Add remaining ingredients. Stir to mix well. Pour over chicken. Cover. Bake in 350°F (180°C) oven for about 1 hour. Serves 6.

STUFFED TURKEY THIGHS

Economical as well as a convenient treat. Cranberry sauce goes well with this.

Turkey thighs	6	6
Envelope stuffing mix, prepared according to directions on box	6 oz.	170 g

Cut around bone to remove meat.

Using about ½ cup (125 mL) stuffing, put it in place of bone. Tie with string or skewer loosely. Put into small roaster. Cover. Roast in 325°F (160°C) oven for about 2 hours until tender. Cut into 2 pieces each to serve. Serves 6.

FAMOUS FRIED CHICKEN

Can there be a longer list of ingredients? Once the seasoning is put together the list is cut in half. This makes excellent fried chicken.

Chicken pieces	3 lbs.	1.35 kg
Water	2 cups	500 mL
Salt	1 tsp.	5 mL
SEASONING		
Paprika	4 tbsp.	60 mL
Dry mustard	2 tbsp.	30 mL
Salt	2 tbsp.	30 mL
Pepper	1 tbsp.	15 mL
Celery salt	1 tbsp.	15 mL
Garlic salt	1 tbsp.	15 mL
Ginger	1 tsp.	5 mL
Thyme	1 tsp.	5 mL
Basil	½ tsp.	2 mL
Oregano	½ tsp.	2 mL
BATTER		
Egg, fork beaten	1	1
Milk	1 cup	250 mL
Flour	1 cup	250 mL
Baking powder	1 tsp.	5 mL
Salt	½ tsp.	2 mL
Pepper	⅛ tsp.	0.5 mL
Prepared seasoning (above)	2 tbsp.	30 mL

Fine dry bread crumbs, for coating
Fat for deep-frying

Put chicken, water and salt into saucepan. Cover. Simmer until tender. Add more water if needed. Drain and cool before dipping into batter.

Seasoning: Measure all ingredients into small bowl. Mix well. Use 2 tbsp. (30 mL) in batter and store remainder in small bottle for future use.

Batter: Mix all 7 ingredients together in order given.

Dip chicken into batter, then into crumbs. Drop into hot fat 375°F (190°C). Deep-fry until brown. Drain on paper towel lined tray. Keep hot in 200°F (110°C) oven while rest is cooking. Serves 3 to 4.

The addition of raisins and pineapple makes for a different and good mixture. Makes a nice gravy.

Small chicken breasts	8	8
Butter or margarine, melted	½ cup	125 mL
Salt, good sprinkle		
Pepper, sprinkle		
SAUCE		
Grated orange rind	1 tbsp.	15 mL
Prepared orange juice	1½ cups	350 mL
Pineapple tidbits with juice	14 oz.	398 mL
Raisins	1 cup	250 mL
Chopped pecans or walnuts	¾ cup	175 mL
Cinnamon	½ tsp.	2 mL
Allspice	¼ tsp.	1 mL
All-purpose flour	2 tbsp.	30 mL
Water	¼ cup	60 mL
Soy sauce	2 tsp.	10 mL
Sliced oranges, for garnish		

Dip meat into melted butter. Place on baking sheet with sides. Sprinkle with salt and pepper. Bake uncovered in 400°F (200°C) oven for 20 minutes. Reduce oven heat to 350°F (180°C).

Sauce: Measure next 7 ingredients into saucepan. Bring to a boil stirring often. Pour over chicken. Bake for 30 minutes more until tender. Transfer meat to platter.

Pour sauce into saucepan. Mix flour, water and soy sauce until smooth. Add to saucepan. Stir over medium heat until it boils and thickens. Pour over meat. Garnish with sliced oranges.

Variation: Sprinkle heavily with curry powder after dipping in melted butter and sprinkling with salt and pepper. Try this on all or even on a few pieces.

Paré Pointer

When a girl needs help don't call her brother. After all, he can't be a brother and assist'er too.

ROAST CHICKEN

There should be a plump chicken on every table every so often.

Roasting chicken	6 lbs.	2.7 kg
NO FUSS STUFFING		
Dry bread crumbs	6 cups	1.25 L
Dry onion flakes	¼ cup	60 mL
Parsley flakes	1 tbsp.	15 mL
Poultry seasoning	2 tsp.	10 mL
Celery salt	½ tsp.	2 mL
Salt	1 tsp.	5 mL
Pepper	¼ tsp.	1 mL
Butter or margarine, melted	¼ cup	60 mL
Water	1½ cups	350 mL

Tie wings close to body with string.

No Fuss Stuffing: Mix first 7 ingredients together in large bowl.

Stir in butter and water. Toss together well. Mixture should be damp enough to retain shape when a handful is squeezed. Add a bit more water if needed. Stuff chicken. Skewer shut. Tie legs to tail. Place in roaster. Cover. Roast in 400°F (200°C) oven for 20 minutes. Reduce heat and roast in 325°F (160°C) oven until tender, about 4 hours more. Joints should move freely. Meat thermometer should read 190°F (90°C). Remove cover last few minutes to brown more if needed. If you prefer to roast uncovered be sure to baste often. Serves 8.

GRAVY		
Chicken fat	½ cup	125 mL
All-purpose flour	½ cup	125 mL
Salt	1 tsp.	5 mL
Pepper	¼ tsp.	1 mL
Drippings plus water	4 cups	1 L

In chicken fat mix in flour, salt and pepper. Whisk in drippings and water over medium heat until it boils and thickens. Taste for salt and pepper. Makes 4 cups (1 L). This allows ½ cup (125 mL) gravy per person for 8 people. Increase ingredients in proportion to make more gravy. Add a bit of gravy browner if needed keeping in mind that chicken gravy is not as dark as beef gravy.

(continued on next page)

PAN STUFFING: Use 2 chicken bouillon cubes with water to make stuffing. Put stuffing into small roaster. Cover with at least ½ cup (125 mL) sliced butter or margarine. Pour about ¾ cup (175 mL) water around outside edge. Cover. Bake in 350°F (180°C) oven for about 30 minutes. Stir after 15 to 20 minutes adding more water if needed.

BREAD STUFFING: Omit onion flakes. Sauté ½ cup (125 mL) each of chopped onion and celery in ¼ cup (60 mL) butter or margarine. Mix with rest of ingredients.

SAUSAGE STUFFING: Add ½ to 1 lb. (225 to 454 g) sausage meat, scramble fried, to Bread Stuffing.

APPLE STUFFING: Add 2 coarsely grated apples to No Fuss Stuffing.

CHICKEN PATTIES

A wonderful variation in poultry for the young crowd and older too.

Boneless raw chicken or turkey, ground	1 lb.	450 g
Fresh mushrooms, minced	1⅓ cups	325 mL
Dry bread crumbs	½ cup	125 mL
Egg	1	1
Salt	1 tsp.	5 mL
Pepper	¼ tsp.	1 mL
Milk (optional)		

Mix all ingredients together in bowl. Add a bit of milk if too dry. Shape into patties. Fry in greased frying pan. Remove meat mixture and keep warm. Make gravy. Makes 9 patties or 24 meatballs.

GRAVY		
All-purpose flour	2 tbsp.	30 mL
Butter or margarine	1 - 2 tbsp.	15 - 30 mL
Salt	½ tsp.	2 mL
Pepper, light sprinkle		
Water	1 cup	250 mL
Gravy browner, as needed		

Mix flour into any remaining bits in frying pan. Add enough butter to moisten flour. Mix in salt and pepper. Stir in water until it boils and thickens. Add a bit of gravy browner if needed. Makes 1 cup (250 mL).

MEASUREMENT TABLES

Throughout this book measurements are given in Conventional and Metric measure. To compensate for differences between the two measurements due to rounding, a full metric measure is not always used. The cup used is the standard 8 fluid ounce. Temperature is given in degrees Fahrenheit and Celsius. Baking pan measurements are in inches and centimetres as well as quarts and litres. An exact metric conversion is given below as well as the working equivalent (Standard Measure).

OVEN TEMPERATURES

Fahrenheit (°F)	Celsius (°C)
175°	80°
200°	95°
225°	110°
250°	120°
275°	140°
300°	150°
325°	160°
350°	175°
375°	190°
400°	205°
425°	220°
450°	230°
475°	240°
500°	260°

SPOONS

Conventional Measure	Metric Exact Conversion Millilitre (mL)	Metric Standard Measure Millilitre (mL)
1/8 teaspoon (tsp.)	0.6 mL	0.5 mL
1/4 teaspoon (tsp.)	1.2 mL	1 mL
1/2 teaspoon (tsp.)	2.4 mL	2 mL
1 teaspoon (tsp.)	4.7 mL	5 mL
2 teaspoons (tsp.)	9.4 mL	10 mL
1 tablespoon (tbsp.)	14.2 mL	15 mL

CUPS

	Metric Exact Conversion	Metric Standard Measure
1/4 cup (4 tbsp.)	56.8 mL	50 mL
1/3 cup (5 1/3 tbsp.)	75.6 mL	75 mL
1/2 cup (8 tbsp.)	113.7 mL	125 mL
2/3 cup (10 2/3 tbsp.)	151.2 mL	150 mL
3/4 cup (12 tbsp.)	170.5 mL	175 mL
1 cup (16 tbsp.)	227.3 mL	250 mL
4 1/2 cups	1022.9 mL	1000 mL (1 L)

PANS

Conventional Inches	Metric Centimetres
8x8 inch	20x20 cm
9x9 inch	22x22 cm
9x13 inch	22x33 cm
10x15 inch	25x38 cm
11x17 inch	28x43 cm
8x2 inch round	20x5 cm
9x2 inch round	22x5 cm
10x4 1/2 inch tube	25x11 cm
8x4x3 inch loaf	20x10x7 cm
9x5x3 inch loaf	22x12x7 cm

DRY MEASUREMENTS

Conventional Measure Ounces (oz.)	Metric Exact Conversion Grams (g)	Metric Standard Measure Grams (g)
1 oz.	28.3 g	30 g
2 oz.	56.7 g	55 g
3 oz.	85.0 g	85 g
4 oz.	113.4 g	125 g
5 oz.	141.7 g	140 g
6 oz.	170.1 g	170 g
7 oz.	198.4 g	200 g
8 oz.	226.8 g	250 g
16 oz.	453.6 g	500 g
32 oz.	907.2 g	1000 g (1 kg)

CASSEROLES (Canada & Britain)

Standard Size Casserole	Exact Metric Measure
1 qt. (5 cups)	1.13 L
1 1/2 qts. (7 1/2 cups)	1.69 L
2 qts. (10 cups)	2.25 L
2 1/2 qts. (12 1/2 cups)	2.81 L
3 qts. (15 cups)	3.38 L
4 qts. (20 cups)	4.5 L
5 qts. (25 cups)	5.63 L

CASSEROLES (United States)

Standard Size Casserole	Exact Metric Measure
1 qt. (4 cups)	900 mL
1 1/2 qts. (6 cups)	1.35 L
2 qts. (8 cups)	1.8 L
2 1/2 qts. (10 cups)	2.25 L
3 qts. (12 cups)	2.7 L
4 qts. (16 cups)	3.6 L
5 qts. (20 cups)	4.5 L

MAIL ORDER FORM
Deduct $5.00 for every $35.00 ordered

Save $5.00

COMPANY'S COMING SERIES

ENGLISH

Quantity		Quantity		Quantity	
	150 Delicious Squares		Vegetables		Microwave Cooking
	Casseroles		Main Courses		Preserves
	Muffins & More		Pasta		Light Casseroles
	Salads		Cakes		Chicken, Etc.
	Appetizers		Barbecues		Kids Cooking
	Desserts		Dinners of the World		Fish & Seafood
	Soups & Sandwiches		Lunches		Breads
	Holiday Entertaining		Pies		*NEW* Meatless Cooking
	Cookies		Light Recipes		*NEW* Cooking For Two (September 1997)

	NO. OF BOOKS	PRICE
FIRST BOOK: $12.99 + $3.00 shipping = $15.99 each x		= $
ADDITIONAL BOOKS: $12.99 + $1.50 shipping = $14.49 each x		= $

PINT SIZE BOOKS

Quantity		Quantity		Quantity	
	Finger Food		Buffets		Chocolate
	Party Planning		Baking Delights		

	NO. OF BOOKS	PRICE
FIRST BOOK: $4.99 + $2.00 shipping = $6.99 each x		= $
ADDITIONAL BOOKS: $4.99 + $1.00 shipping = $5.99 each x		= $

JEAN PARÉ LIVRES DE CUISINE

FRENCH

Quantity		Quantity		Quantity	
	150 délicieux carrés		Recettes légères		La cuisine pour les enfants
	Les casseroles		Les salades		Poissons et fruits de mer
	Muffins et plus		La cuisson au micro-ondes		Les pains
	Les dîners		Les pâtes		*NEW* La cuisine sans viande
	Les barbecues		Les conserves		*NEW* La cuisine pour deux (septembre1997)
	Les tartes		Les casseroles légères		
	Délices des fêtes		Poulet, etc.		

	NO. OF BOOKS	PRICE
FIRST BOOK: $12.99 + $3.00 shipping = $15.99 each x		= $
ADDITIONAL BOOKS: $12.99 + $1.50 shipping = $14.49 each x		= $

TOTAL

- **MAKE CHEQUE OR MONEY ORDER PAYABLE TO:** *COMPANY'S COMING PUBLISHING LIMITED*
- **ORDERS OUTSIDE CANADA:** *Must be paid in U.S. funds by cheque or money order drawn on Canadian or U.S. bank.*
- *Prices subject to change without prior notice.*
- *Sorry, no C.O.D.'s*

TOTAL PRICE FOR ALL BOOKS	$
Less $5.00 for every $35.00 ordered −	$
SUBTOTAL	$
Canadian residents add G.S.T. +	$
TOTAL AMOUNT ENCLOSED	$

Please complete shipping address on reverse.

Gift Giving

- Let us help you with your gift giving!

- We will send cookbooks directly to the recipients of your choice if you give us their names and addresses.

- Be sure to specify the titles you wish to send to each person.

- If you would like to include your personal note or card, we will be pleased to enclose it with your gift order.

- Company's Coming Cookbooks make excellent gifts. Birthdays, bridal showers, Mother's Day, Father's Day, graduation or any occasion... collect them all!

Shipping address

Send the Company's Coming Cookbooks listed on the reverse side of this coupon, to:

Name:

Street:

City: Province/State:

Postal Code/Zip: Tel: (   )   —

COOKBOOKS

Company's Coming Publishing Limited
Box 8037, Station F
Edmonton, Alberta, Canada T6H 4N9
Tel: (403) 450-6223
Fax: (403) 450-1857

Cookmark

Complete your collection.

Look for these *Best-Sellers* where you shop!

All New Recipes

Sample Recipe from
Cooking For Two

COQ AU VIN

This excellent variation is out of the ordinary to be sure.

Hard margarine (butter browns too fast)	1 tbsp.	15 mL
Chicken parts, skin (removed)	4-5	4-5
All-purpose flour	¼ cup	60 mL
Sliced onion	½ cup	125 mL
Canned tomatoes, mashed	14 oz.	398 mL
Canned whole mushrooms, drained	10 oz.	284 mL
Bay leaf	1	1
Garlic powder	⅛ tsp.	0.5 mL
Granulated sugar	¼ tsp.	1 mL
Salt, sprinkle		
Pepper, sprinkle		
Red wine (or alcohol-free wine)	¼ cup	60 mL

Melt margarine in frying pan. Dip chicken in flour. Brown both sides of chicken in frying pan. Transfer to ungreased 1½ quart (1.5 L) casserole.

Add onion to frying pan. Sauté until browned.

Add next 7 ingredients to onion. Stir. Cook slowly for 5 minutes. Discard bay leaf.

Stir in wine. Pour over chicken. Cover. Bake in 325°F (160°C) oven for 1 to 1½ hours until tender. Serves 2.

Use this handy checklist to complete your collection of
Company's Coming Cookbooks